Brooklyn's Famous Eating Place

JOE'S RESTAURANT • 326-334 Fulton Street, Brooklyn, New York

2107— *Temple Bar and Dime Saving's Bank Buildings*
BROOKLYN.

Brooklyn Bound!

Greetings from Brooklyn

The Great Cables on Brooklyn Bridge, N. Y. City

Randall Gabrielan

Schiffer Publishing Ltd

4880 Lower Valley Road • Atglen, PA • 19310

Fulton Street — Heart of the Shopping District, Brooklyn, N.Y.

Other Schiffer Books by the Author:

Jersey City: A Monumental History,
978-0-7643-2638-7, $24.95
Middletown, Monmouth County, New Jersey,
978-0-7643-2918-0, $24.99
Long Branch, New Jersey: Remembering a Resort,
978-0-7643-3366-8, $24.99
Hoboken: History and Architecture at a Glance,
978-0-7643-3652-2, $29.99

Schiffer Books are available at special discounts for bulk purchases for sales promotions or premiums. Special editions, including personalized covers, corporate imprints, and excerpts can be created in large quantities for special needs. For more information contact the publisher:

Published by Schiffer Publishing Ltd.
4880 Lower Valley Road
Atglen, PA 19310
Phone: (610) 593-1777; Fax: (610) 593-2002
E-mail: Info@schifferbooks.com

For the largest selection of fine reference books on this and related subjects, please visit our website at:
www.schifferbooks.com

We are always looking for people to write books on new and related subjects. If you have an idea for a book, please contact us at proposals@schifferbooks.com.

This book may be purchased from the publisher.
Include $5.00 for shipping.
Please try your bookstore first.
You may write for a free catalog.

In Europe, Schiffer books are distributed by
Bushwood Books
6 Marksbury Ave.
Kew Gardens
Surrey TW9 4JF England
Phone: 44 (0) 20 8392 8585; Fax: 44 (0) 20 8392 9876
E-mail: info@bushwoodbooks.co.uk
Website: www.bushwoodbooks.co.uk

Contents

Acknowledgments

This book was made possible by the generous contributions of a number of friends and collectors, especially Joan Kay, the dean of the world of Brooklyn postcards. Indeed, the four most repeated words in this work are "Courtesy of Joan Kay."

John Rhody and Robert Pellegrini have assisted with many of the author's books and are represented here. Bob also provided a major assist as driving companion on trips to Brooklyn.

Thanks, too, to the contributors of one or more images, including Barbara Booz, Moe Cuocci, the late Gary Dubnik, Mimi Fride, Stanley Lipson, the late Harold Solomon, and Glenn Vogel.

Introduction

The "large letter" postcard has been a favorite of publishers since the earliest years of the postcard boom. Perhaps their most effective usage was in the linen era when the contours of the letters often contained local imagery. This card is a modern interpretation that incorporates Brooklyn's greatest iconic symbol, one published by Brooklyn Tourism, an initiative of Brooklyn Borough President Marty Markowitz and Best of Brooklyn, Inc.

survey of Brooklyn through post card and other imagery in relatively few pages is daunting enough, but introducing this city, now borough, and the world of post cards in two pages permits only brief and highlighted references. Brooklyn's position at the western end of Long Island is a geographical position that has loomed large in the city's development and history. While settled about concurrently with Manhattan, the separation of Brooklyn from Manhattan by water proved a barrier that would keep Brooklyn a small town until bridges literally paved the way for its expansion and trolleys lines were built to facilitate the transport of its residents to every corner of the expansive county. Brooklyn as farming community has been well-documented. Vestiges of its agricultural past survived into the mid-twentieth century, while a small number of former farm houses have managed to survive.

Brooklyn was organized in the seventeenth century, comprised of the English town of Gravesend, five Dutch towns of Brooklyn, Flatbush, Flatlands, Bushwick, and New Utrecht. Original Brooklyn proper was a relatively small part clustered near the ferries that "connected" it to the earlier developed island of Manhattan. Thus, Kings was a county of independent municipalities long before it became one county in a city of five consolidated counties in 1898. That year is also significant in the postcard world, for the passage of the Private Mailing Card Act. The Private Mailing Card Act began the popularization of postcards that accelerated in the early years of the twentieth century and became a collecting craze in the years between 1905 and 1915, when the postcard also served as a common speedy communication means.

Early non-agrarian northern Brooklyn also developed a maritime trade and industry along its waterfront, most notably its famed navy yard. Southern parts were home to many resorts that thrived in the pre-trolley period. If one were to analyze a single factor to trace Brooklyn's growth, the most telling would be the expansion of rapid transit, initially both elevated and surface lines, and the streetcars that became synonymous with the city. News accounts of the late nineteenth and early twentieth centuries are replete with accounts of evolving rail access becoming the fulcrum for new developments making Brooklyn a city of neighborhoods. These neighborhoods had boundaries that shifted or changed with time, settlement practices and demographic change. Brooklyn was known as the city of churches at least since the second quarter of the nineteenth century with worship practice providing a second identity of locale, especially during the ascendency and predominance of the Roman Catholic Church. Old-timers recall the time when they, and even some contemporaries, defined their origin or residency by their parish rather than neighborhood. This could be a tighter definition of territory as densely packed neighborhoods include multiple parishes. Neighborhood identity changes from identification of new ones, e.g. Dumbo, a new appellation for a gentrified old industrial area, or the distinction of smaller places, e.g. Ditmas Park, which, although it was defined from its establishment over a century ago, for many decades it fell under the general rubric of Flatbush. Or, in some cases, distinct areas may be identified within their larger surrounds, such as the many in Fort Hamilton that think of themselves as part of Bay Ridge.

Brooklyn has undergone major demographic shifts and commercial change in recent decades. The city is well-known as a home for immigrants during the massive influx of overseas settlers in the latter nineteenth and early twentieth centuries. Some of those peoples established neighborhoods that became celebrated for their tight-knit ethnicity. While many of the children and grandchildren of these settlers headed for the suburbs, they were replaced by waves of new peoples from other lands who replicated the experience. Some traditional neighborhoods have shrunk, while other ethnics have expanded their holds. Brooklyn once had a strong manufacturing base, but it, as has much of the industrial north, has evaporated. A number of these regions that have lost their commercial anchors are among the most vibrant places of change. They were often raised to new vitality by the familiar process of resettled artists who sought inexpensive space moving in and revitalizing cultural life. Some, as the aforementioned Dumbo, have adaptively reused existing structures to house the new population while others, such as Williamsburg, have had numbers, types and sizes of new construction that would have been unthinkable a mere two decades ago.

Much of the dual histories of tradition and change is shown through the postcard medium, which as noted earlier, was at its most popular during Brooklyn's post-consolidation great growth period. A basic postcard primer will be helpful to the non-post card audience that tends to read these books. The majority of the cards in this book (and in existence) are from the so-called "golden age" of postcards, which the author defines as 1905-1915. Most are given a date estimate in the caption, but they are often detectable by their old look, including that of the subject matter, and their graphic quality. Many were produced in Europe by a printing industry that was well-ahead of its American counterpart at that time. Some publishers, including entrepreneurial photographers, made actual photographs into postcards by printing on postcard paper stock. These cards, with abbreviated reference as "real photos" are among the most desirable collecting varieties at publication. The tilting of the market in the 1912 or so period to the inferior American made product, which resulted from a number of factors including protective tariffs, contributed to the decline of collector interest of a craze that may also have just run its course.

The year 1915 also ushered in the next definable phase of the picture postcard — the "white border" era — that was current for about fifteen years, its product readily detectable by the white border that ran along all four edges, which some attribute to an ink savings technique, and their generally inferior graphic quality. Some older cards were reprinted in the white border process. Comparing examples of both will illustrate just how dismal postcards became during this time. White border cards still do not get respect. The short, unhappy life of the white border was superseded around 1930 by the so-called "linen card," which resulted from a new postcard paper that was able to absorb new inks which enabled new coloration techniques on stock that often had a raised surface and a feel not unlike linen. While at one time linens also lacked respect, certain types have become eagerly sought because of coloration and interesting pictorial content, among them diners, retail stores and a variety of colorful advertising subjects. Linens were predominant during the 1930s, but started sharing the market with its successor, the "chrome" card, which was introduced around 1940. Chrome is an abbreviation for photochrome, so called because they resembled photographs; early examples were produced from a new film of the era, Kodak's outstanding Kodachrome, to some, the greatest color film ever made. The linens predominated in the 1940s, but the chromes had seized most of the market by 1950. Indeed, to find a late 1950s linen is a rarity. Other printing types were utilized for cards, including black and whites that are not categorized, but this description is intended only as an overview. In addition, there is one distinguishing character of the eras of cards not mentioned, but often not detectable in a book, the 1960s introduction of chrome cards larger than the traditional 3.5 x 5.5 inches. These are called "continentals" since this size card was developed on the European continent. They, too, get no collector respect. Since postcards have slipped as a contemporary communications medium, relatively few new chromes are produced, especially for Brooklyn.

The author's selection of imagery often weighed and compared the interest (value) of the card itself versus the subject matter portrayed. The less-appealing card was at times chosen, frequently as a matter of necessity if the long view of history was to be presented. For example, some of Brooklyn's significant buildings were erected during the white border period of dismal graphic quality cards. In addition, the modern chrome cards hardly get any respect, but they, too, are critical for linking a streetscape familiar to the current reader with the historical past. The cards are supplemented by contemporary photographs in order to bring history up to date and, in a few cases, where the contemporary image was so much more effective than the old card it replaced.

Old Brooklyn

Brooklyn historically is the relatively small part of Kings County that is in the area around the old ferries, along with the present downtown and Brooklyn Heights. While the book's rough geographic organization does not link places by virtue of the old town division of seventeenth century Kings County, this chapter consists of Brooklyn Heights, the Brooklyn Bridge area and Dumbo, along with Downtown and small neighborhoods adjoining the Heights. The bridge is a likely place to begin the volume because, for practical purposes, the Brooklyn Bridge marked the start of the maturing of Brooklyn. The bridge and Brooklyn's street cars created an opportunity for Brooklyn to become competitive with Manhattan as a residential base that would appeal to the former's office and professional workers.

A business center developed in the downtown area, where the courts and county records operation were removed from Flatbush after downtown became the county seat. The old Brooklyn chapter also includes the city's early prestigious residential district, Brooklyn Heights, which after surviving a near-precipitous slip in the post World War II years, was revitalized to retain its former standing as an outstanding area to live.

chapter one
Brooklyn Bridge

The bridge was approved in April 1867, but the start of construction suffered delays and an additional setback after Roebling died in a ferry accident in June 1869. Work finally began in 1870. Roebling's son, Washington, carried on, solving numerous engineering problems, but he was disabled in 1872 by a case of the bends suffered while working with his men in the construction of the foundation. The first wire on the 85-foot wide bridge was run out May 29, 1877. Construction was watched avidly, reported regularly, and illustrated on these stereograph cards, which served as both popular entertainment and news photographs. The completed span of 1,595-1/2 feet made this at the time the longest suspension bridge in the world. Glimpses of the ferry and Brooklyn's enormous sugar plant are in the right and left respectively.

3168. Brooklyn, from pier of the Suspension Bridge, New York.

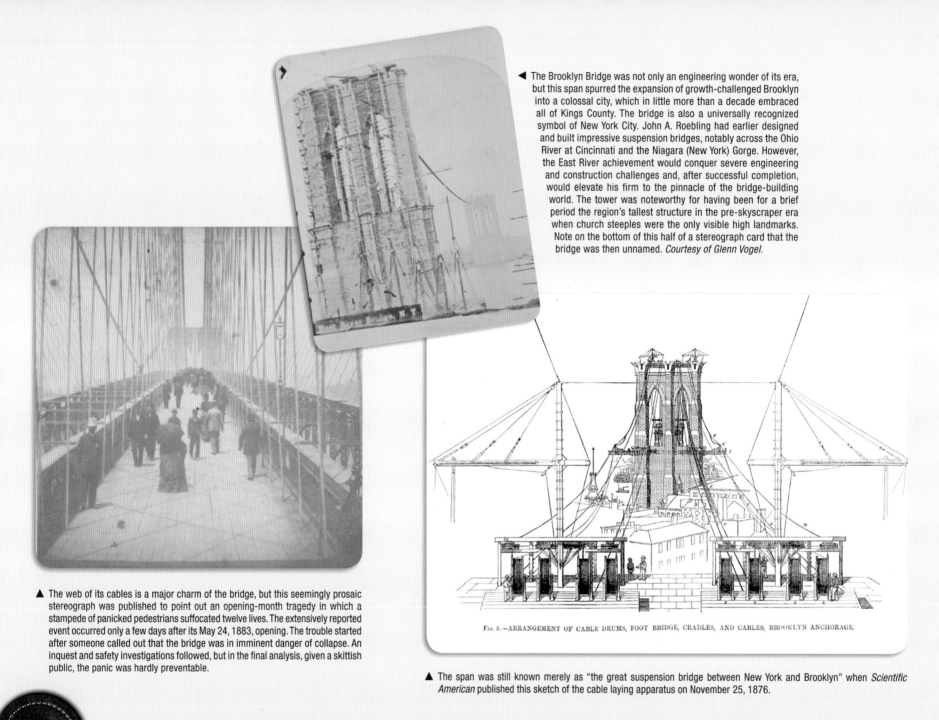

The Brooklyn Bridge was not only an engineering wonder of its era, but this span spurred the expansion of growth-challenged Brooklyn into a colossal city, which in little more than a decade embraced all of Kings County. The bridge is also a universally recognized symbol of New York City. John A. Roebling had earlier designed and built impressive suspension bridges, notably across the Ohio River at Cincinnati and the Niagara (New York) Gorge. However, the East River achievement would conquer severe engineering and construction challenges and, after successful completion, would elevate his firm to the pinnacle of the bridge-building world. The tower was noteworthy for having been for a brief period the region's tallest structure in the pre-skyscraper era when church steeples were the only visible high landmarks. Note on the bottom of this half of a stereograph card that the bridge was then unnamed. *Courtesy of Glenn Vogel.*

FIG. 8.—ARRANGEMENT OF CABLE DRUMS, FOOT BRIDGE, CRADLES, AND CABLES, BROOKLYN ANCHORAGE.

The web of its cables is a major charm of the bridge, but this seemingly prosaic stereograph was published to point out an opening-month tragedy in which a stampede of panicked pedestrians suffocated twelve lives. The extensively reported event occurred only a few days after its May 24, 1883, opening. The trouble started after someone called out that the bridge was in imminent danger of collapse. An inquest and safety investigations followed, but in the final analysis, given a skittish public, the panic was hardly preventable.

The span was still known merely as "the great suspension bridge between New York and Brooklyn" when *Scientific American* published this sketch of the cable laying apparatus on November 25, 1876.

The Great Cables on Brooklyn Bridge, N. Y. City

◄ The main cables were over-engineered to support about five times the weight of the roadway and vehicles. Each of the four main cables is about sixteen inches in diameter and contain nineteen strands, each consisting of about 280 wires. Bridge promenade traffic was enormous in its early years, but had declined over the decades and then soared again during the 1966 subway strike. Brooklyn residents who carpooled to proximity of the bridge found the walk over the river a novel and even, in the author's recollection, an enjoyable experience. The usually crowded Manhattan streets were jammed with an overflow of motor vehicles, so this pedestrian flow helped avoid total gridlock. The bridge has since regained its attraction as a popular walkway. The card is an appealing soft color Rotograph, c.1905.

Samuel Chamberlain, a skilled and prolific photographer, ► left an oeuvre that numbers many books of his pictures, primarily New England subjects. He also published, c.1930s-40s, a long series of sepia postcards titled *The American Scene*, which numbers several New York City views, including No. 390, Brooklyn Bridge. While stating little about the bridge, the card effectively conveys the image of a tough, gritty Brooklyn waterfront.

COPR DETROIT PHOTOGRAPHIC CO.

8067 BROOKLYN BRIDGE, NEW YORK.   TOTAL LENGTH 5990 FEET   PIERS 1595 FEET

▲ The mix of business and residential buildings in close proximity to the bridge is illustrated on a c.1900 Detroit Publishing card. This publisher sometimes used photographs taken a few years prior to the card's publication. The northern ends of these two streets, Furman (closer to the water) and Columbia Heights, were extensively disturbed, first for the construction of the Squibb factory buildings and later for the erection of the Brooklyn-Queens Expressway. Note the tall mansard, which denotes the former ferry building.

QUAKER OATS

Brooklyn Bridge.   New York.

◄ Bridge traffic increased enormously, first with the cable cars that crossed the bridge by September 1883 and followed by the electric trolley service that began in 1898. The rails were vital, if not fundamental, to the growth of Brooklyn. The ability to cross the bridge by trolley enhanced residential Brooklyn's appeal to New York businessmen. Brooklyn's rents were lower than Manhattan's while Bronx residents found the short trolley ride more convenient than the elevated railroad.

Brooklyn Bridge from Brooklyn, N. Y.

◄ A northwest Brooklyn Heights scene a short distance south of the previous view is recognizable in 2010 due to the row of intact houses on the west side of Columbia Heights and the presence in the image of the no-longer extant, but historically significant, Hotel Margaret. The five-story, redbrick double house, with the pointed cornice, near left bottom at number 148-150 and the four houses to its north still stand. The two houses adjacent on the south are gone; their lots are now the entrance to the Promenade. The two houses at the bottom were replaced by an apartment building.

chapter two

Brooklyn Heights

Busy docks, ample storage facilities, and streets able to handle cargo traffic prompted enthusiastic Brooklyn optimism over its maritime future that the Brooklyn Daily Eagle could assert October 12, 1897, at the dawn of consolidation: "Brooklyn (as) no city in the world can present such an imposing line of water front accommodations, where ships from every clime can be docked and have their cargos disposed of with a single handling. A fifteen mile stretch of water boundary at any point of which deep sea going ships may tie up, fringed by enormous storage accommodations and manufacturing establishments, at many places extending blocks inland, from Gravesend Bay north and cast in unbroken occupancy to Long Island Sound, is indeed a feature of a great city worthy of the pride its excites." History would repeat itself, although in a twisted reversal of fortune.

NEW YORK SKYSCRAPERS AS SEEN FROM BROOKLYN, NEW YORK.

The docks are pictured not long ▶ after they were reconstructed in a massive several-year project that began in the late 1950s. However, local shipping was already doomed as the by then congested Brooklyn docks could neither anticipate nor subsequently handle the evolving industry. Note the ships' cranes, used to handle break-bulk or loose cargo. There vessels were already on their way to obsolescence, as the first container ports were emerging in Port Newark on the New Jersey side of the bay. Not only did Brooklyn not have the larger area such facilities required, but also its streets were now congested and its location on the western tip of Long Island was not conducive to inland shipment. Brooklyn Bridge Park is under development at the pictured scene.

▲ Brooklyn industry thrived through World War II, but as its waterfront aged, its docks became inadequate for post-war shipping. The Port Authority of New York (before they added New Jersey to their name) undertook a costly seven-year redevelopment plan, rebuilding the docks and warehouse facilities. Those fond of dating postcards by the built environment will not find a hint on the New York side, where nothing of substance was erected from the mid-1930s to the 1960 Chase Manhattan Bank tower, built well after publication of this chrome card. However, the foreground suggests the year is 1947 in view of the topping out of the ten-story Bethel Home of the Jehovah's Witnesses at 124 Columbia Heights.

◀ While the New York preservation movement matured with the 1963 demolition of the Pennsylvania Station, the destructive potential of civic construction had been manifested in the 1940s with the first announced plans for the Brooklyn-Queens Expressway. The intended roadway followed a course that would have cut the heart out of Brooklyn Heights. The local uproar not only resulted in a compromise, but also the construction of one of the greatest urban pedestrian amenities: the Esplanade atop the three-level road, in which the two lower ones handle vehicular traffic in each direction. The c.1950 card, the era of the round-corner chrome, was published by the Jehovah's Witnesses to show the newly completed Bethel Home.

BROOKLYN AND WILLIAMSBURG BRIDGES, NEW YORK CITY   20

14814

▲ Dr. Edward R. Squibb, who developed a better, safer way of making ether and opened a Brooklyn factory in 1858, founded a pharmaceutical giant that at its centennial made eighty-five percent of the ether in the country. They moved to New Jersey in 1969, claiming their Brooklyn plant was outmoded for their purposes. However, the sprawling complex near the river soon became a satisfactory home to the Jehovah's Witnesses. One can still pass through the two former Squibb factory buildings at the left on Columbia Heights, but be mindful that the walk up the hill is slow and difficult in a manner not imagined while going down. However, much of the remainder of this c.1940 linen card image was destroyed for the construction of the Brooklyn-Queens Expressway. The docks are gone while Willow and Hicks, the two north-south streets at left and right respectively, were truncated.

Plans to build a park on the site of abandoned piers and warehouses had been discussed for a decade, with construction beginning in earnest in 2009 for the Brooklyn Bridge Park. At completion, a green belt will run from the edge of the bridge to Atlantic Avenue. The last of the Furman Street warehouses, number 66, is pictured on June 11, 2010, shortly prior to demolition for park construction. The greenery at left shows an open early section near the river. The tip of the Empire State Building is visible over the doomed structure.

In three decades, the region surrounding both sides of the Manhattan Bridge went from seedy industrial to emerging artistic to historic district. Locals coined its now widely known acronym Dumbo, for "Down Under the Manhattan Bridge Overpass." However, when they did so in 1978, they hoped this self-effacing, even derisive nickname would dissuade developers. Experience proved otherwise. The center of this c.1990s aerial is dominated by the Gair buildings while the old Fulton ferry area is discernible at the left. The Consolidated Edison power station is on the right.

While plans for the Manhattan Bridge were approved in November 1899, two changes in design, including one that reversed the earlier, delayed construction. A change of architects resulted in Carrere and Hastings redesigning the bridge's huge anchorages. A view of the massive Brooklyn anchorage, virtually hidden in plain view, inspires awe. It contains around 115,000 cubic yards of concrete and weighs nearly 223,000 tons, although the numbers may be meaningless to all but the few who can measure construction materials. The card, which dates from the later construction period, was published by Heidelberg Portland Cement Company as part of a series featuring structures in which their product was used.

The Manhattan Bridge, engineered by Gustave Lindenthal, was for years referred to as Bridge Number 3, which now denotes its aesthetic ranking among the lower East River trio. Note the colonnade at top, which the architects claimed was intended to alert travelers that they had reached the anchorage section and provide a covered place of rest. The Manhattan, after it opened to the public on December 31, 1909, relieved congestion on the Brooklyn Bridge, but only for a short time. Engineers now know that traffic increases with access to new roads.

◀ This 1970s chrome card was published by the Jehovah's Witnesses to show off their growing Brooklyn Heights holdings. The area in front of No. 6, the former Squibb factory that was then an office complex, permits the viewer to perceive the destruction of surrounding buildings depicted in the nearby c.1940 linen. The No. 1 Bethel Home residence is also pictured under construction in a view of the harbor. The buildings along that street are the western elevations of the west side of Columbia Heights structures. No. 4, the 1889-built Hotel Margaret, was destroyed in a fire in 1980. The finely preserved No. 5, the former 1928 Leverich Tower Hotel, stands at the northeast corner of Willow and Clark Streets while the huge St. George complex, which is not part of the Jehovah's Witness' holdings, is behind it. Other residences and their factory complex, No. 7 at 117 Adams Street, complete the image.

▼ Some of the buildings in the prior sequence can be seen looking west. In addition, the impact of the Expressway's cutting off Dumbo is well-illustrated in this c.1980 view. The section in the lower right corner conveys a grittiness that long-characterized pre-gentrification Dumbo. The greenery in the left middle is the northern reach of Cadman Plaza. A colonnade and anchorage of the Manhattan Bridge can also be spotted. At publication, the Jehovah's Witnesses are engaged in the lengthy process of divesting their Brooklyn Heights holdings — an action that will complete a move to upstate New York.

▲ Gairville was the century-old identity of the core of present-day Dumbo, a designation that stemmed from the extensive local cardboard box manufacturing plants of Robert Gair, who relocated here from lower Manhattan around the late 1880s. He died in 1927 at about the time his firm was leaving the city. Perhaps he would have been forgotten, but he built a series of connected concrete factories, each numbered and marked with his name. Gair Building No. 6, on the right, stands at the northwest corner of Washington and Front Streets. Building No. 7 was built in 1914 at Main Street between Water and Plymouth Streets and is now houses residential condominiums; it is the best known of the buildings, but its new identity is the Clocktower. The view from the Brooklyn Bridge shows the Brooklyn-Queens Expressway in the foreground, a roadway that contributed to the area's industrial decline by cutting it off from the rest of Brooklyn.

Stiles published this view of the foot of Fulton Street in order to illustrate the Hetfield & Duckers Cracker plant at the left. However, the principal interest of the image a century and a quarter later is for an extant landmark — the Long Island Safe Deposit Company at the right — seen in its ancient streetscape at the approach to the ferry. Today it is a key structure in the Fulton Ferry Historic District, which was entered on the National Register in 1974. The now-preserved brick buildings to its west, which date from the 1830s, fell into a state of seediness after the ferry ceased operation in 1924.

The cast iron Long Island Safe Deposit Company bank building, designed by William Mundell, was built 1868-9 at 1 Front Street, at Old Fulton Street. Its once favorable location a block from the ferry was taken away by the Brooklyn Bridge, visible in the background, which impacted travel patterns. The subsequent reduction in traffic led to their closing in 1891. Now home to a bar/restaurant, the finely restored interior has been used as a setting for a number of movie scenes.

A dock at the Old Fulton Ferry district can lead one to mistake the tower building as the old ferry terminal, which can be discerned in the accompanying engraving. This building was Marine Company No. 7 of the New York City Fire Department; the tower was utilized to dry hose. A Jehovah's Witnesses building and the Eagle Warehouse are left and right respectively. *Courtesy of Robert Pellegrini.*

The Brooklyn Daily Eagle building had earlier stood at 28 Old Fulton Street, the site where the Eagle Warehouse & Storage Company built this warehouse facility in 1893. Brooklyn's Frank Freeman is the architect of the rugged, striking Romanesque design. This picture was taken in 2010 — three decades after its residential conversion by architect Bernard Rothzeid. Note the lettering over the arched entry and under the cornice, the latter separated by a glass clock face.

▼ Grace Court is a one-block street that runs west from Hicks to the river and is named for Grace Church, which is on the southwest corner. Grace Court Alley, which is slightly offset to the north, runs east nearly a full block towards Henry Street. The quaint street of converted stables and carriage houses, which served the Remsen Street houses that adjoined on the north, was pictured in 1990. It is, perhaps, the most charming of the several Heights mews, or narrow paths, that provides a palpable link to the gas-light era.

▲ The Francis Guy painting *Winter Scene in Brooklyn*, the quintessential, even iconic, image of early downtown Brooklyn, is a pleasing landscape, a charming snow scene, and a historical document of one of Brooklyn's earliest built-up areas. Guy (1760-1820), a self-trained artist and immigrant from England, painted this scene, a section of Front Street between Main and Fulton Streets, from his window c.1819-20. One of multiple replicas, it was previously in the collection of the Brooklyn Institute, which saw that it became one of the earliest acquisitions of the Brooklyn Museum. This 58.75" x 75" canvas was damaged by fire and is missing about eighteen inches on its left. The accuracy of the depicted buildings and even the small figures is what gives this remarkable image its historical significance. A detailed description appears in Stiles' *Brooklyn Vol. 2* (pgs. 99-105).

◄ Middagh Street, which has multiple possible Dutch namesakes, lies at the northerly bounds of the Heights, where it is cutoff at the west by the Brooklyn-Queens Expressway. This 2 1/2-story gambrel-roofed Federal residence, pictured in 1990, was originally the c.1820s Eugene Boisselet House and is arguably the finest ancient frame dwelling in the Heights. The three-story brick place adjacent at number 26 dates from the same period.

◀ Multiple frame houses on the east side of Henry Street, numbers 143-7, between Pierrepont and Clark Streets, as seen in 1990, provide a well-preserved reminder of pre-masonry Heights construction.

Two Gutzon Borglum sculptures in the rear of the church's garden court are visible ▶ from the street. The Lincoln in relief was dedicated May 30, 1915, a gift from the Fort Greene Chapter Daughters of the American Revolution in memory of Mrs. S. V. White. The ten-foot statue of Beecher was made around 1910 and dedicated October 19, 1914. The two adjacent figures represent an event at the church in 1860 when Beecher bought the freedom of a slave girl by an "auction" among the congregation. Borglum is best known for the stone faces of four presidents that are carved into Mount Rushmore in South Dakota.

▲ Plymouth Church, one of Brooklyn's oldest and most venerable houses of worship, was designed by Joseph C. Wells and built in 1849 on the north side of Orange Street between Henry and Hicks Streets. At the time, Plymouth, one of the city's largest halls, was used for a variety of public gatherings. The church was so closely identified with celebrated clergy Henry Ward Beecher that his name appears in the identifying slogan on the bottom of this c.1910 card. The building has been little-changed, although the entrance was rebuilt, while the adjacent houses on both sides are gone; the one on the left was replaced by a garden court. Following a 1934 merger with the Congregational Church of the Pilgrims, the organization is now known as the Plymouth Church of the Pilgrims. It was entered on the National Register of Historic Places in 1966.

PACKER FEMALE COLLEGIATE INSTITUTE.

◀ The original Packer Collegiate Institute, a Gothic Revival design of Minard Lafever, one of his last works, was built in 1853-6. The domed tower is on Joralemon Street (no. 170), indicating that the garden entrance fronted Livingston Street. The engraving pre-dates the 1886 extension made behind the tree at right.

Architect Frank Freeman's Richardsonian Romanesque design for the Herman Behr mansion, completed in 1889 at 82 Pierrepont Street at Henry Street, has long been esteemed as one of his finest residential commissions. The building has endured a checkered past, devolving into the Palm Hotel, but later elevated as a Franciscan brothers' residence prior to its conversion to apartments in 1977. While too much of Freeman's oeuvre has been destroyed, this premier example, following a façade restoration, glistens, notably in the morning sun.

Two dwellings near one another depict "in transition" Brooklyn Heights' housing around the second quarter of the nineteenth century. The older one, the frame at 73 Pineapple Street, retains its six-over-six windows, reflecting its Greek Revival origins. It is an infrequent five-bay, three-story house of its time and height, which leads one to wonder if an earlier, smaller house had been expanded. The masonry four-story at 115 Columbia Heights reflects the brick fabric that would become the area's standard. Its windows have been changed, perhaps in the Victorian-era when the fine bay window was added on the Pineapple Street elevation.

The Mansion House, seen on a ▶ c.1905 Rotograph card in its hotel incarnation, has a varied past. Lancaster reported its origins as an 1822 residence prior to service as the Brooklyn Collegiate Institute for Young Ladies, preceding remodeling as a hotel. While the card is stamped "rear view," the building's configuration resembles the present street view of the six-story Mansion House apartments. They were built in the 1930s at 145 Hicks Street.

◀ Built in 1889 at 97 Columbia Heights, at the northeast corner of Orange Street, and designed by Frank Freeman, the Hotel Margaret was the area's first high-rise hotel and one of its finest. Note the sheet metal panels surrounding many windows, which were said to give the place a nautical look. Following purchase by the Jehovah's Witnesses, the Margaret was destroyed by fire in 1980 near the end of an extensive renovation. While then-current construction regulations banned high-rise buildings in New York City's first historic district, the owners pleaded financial hardship based on the economic model of their acquisition, which was dependent on a larger-than-permitted structure. The frame buildings on the southeast corner were replaced by brownstones within a few years of this c.1905 card; they in turn were replaced in 1960 by a Jehovah's Witnesses high-rise residence that pre-dated the regulations established following the 1965 historic district designation of Brooklyn Heights.

HOTEL MARGARET, BROOKLYN, N. Y.

▲ Capt. William Tumbridge began his Hotel St. George in 1885 with a ten-story building (left of the center structure), a section that was rebuilt following its destruction in a 1995 fire. The building topped by the sign was an 1898 addition that faced Clark Street. By the time of its 1903 expansion, or the section at far left, the St. George claimed over 1,000 rooms. Following Tumbridge's 1921 death, the building at the right, on the corner of Henry Street, was designed by Emery Roth and erected in 1923, the approximate date of this white border card.

The focus of this 1930s linen is the tower building, also designed by Emery Roth, ▶ which, after its 1930 completion, elevated the St. George to the city's largest hotel with a total of 2,632 rooms. The enormous complex filled the entire block boarded by Hicks and Henry Streets on the west and east and Pineapple and Clark Streets on the north and south. The card's advertising was directed to a Manhattan clientele that would be rushed here through proximity to the city and speed of the subway. Even the Clark Street station was on-site. The subway, the 2 and 3 trains in modern parlance, is deeper than the artistic license of the card suggests. Passengers are raised from the depths by a station elevator. After the St. George's checkered existence into the early twenty-first century, recent development has divided the former hospitality colossus into several residential properties.

HOTEL ST. GEORGE — CLARK STREET — BROOKLYN, N. Y.

CLARK ST. EXPRESS STATION
7th Ave. I. R. T. Subway
Wall St. 4 Minutes
Times Square 15 Minutes

▲ The Cranlyn, a twelve-story, 150-family apartment building at 80 Pineapple Street, its southwest corner with Henry Street, was designed by H. I. Feldman. It was built on the site of the 1825 Apprentices Library, an antecedent of the Brooklyn Institute of Arts and Sciences and the Brooklyn Public Library. The building, known for its rich, Art Deco decorations, is represented by a metal plaque and a glazed terra-cotta bas-relief that are mounted on the Pineapple Street façade.

▲ ► In the olden days, Montague Street sloped to a ferry terminal on the river. The arch, known informally as the Penny Bridge (right, part of an old print), a not-uncommon bridge nickname, crossed at the present Montague Terrace terminus of Montague Street. The topography was rearranged for the construction of the Brooklyn-Queens Expressway and the Promenade, the walkway now entered at bottom left. The building that possesses the conical tower, 62 Montague Street, ties the much-changed streetscape, pictured on a c.1910 card, to the contemporary scene.

The Bossert's sparkling lobby reflects the extent and quality ▶ of the restoration work. The former hotel is a residence for group members, but it is on the market in 2010 as part of the Witnesses' divestiture of its Brooklyn Heights holdings.

▼ The Queen Anne style Montague, an apartment house designed by the Parfitt Bros. for developer William Ziegler, was completed around 1889, a time when high-rise buildings were gaining favor in Brooklyn. At that time, the Montague was said to have been the most advanced in the city. The *Brooklyn Eagle* card reflects its early twentieth century conversion to an apartment hotel. The building's fortunes, having slipped with the mid-twentieth century fall from fashion of Brooklyn Heights, reached its nadir with the 1952 removal of tenants due to fire code violations. The slow recovery is reflected by its status two decades later as a welfare hotel.

HOTEL BOSSERT,
BROOKLYN

◀ Designed by Helme & Huberty and completed in 1913, the twelve-story Renaissance Revival Hotel Bossert at 98 Montague Street, the southeast corner of Hicks Street, enjoyed a long run as the pinnacle of Brooklyn public hospitality. Its immediate success was reflected by its expansion to full-block length, designed by the same firm, three years later. The original building extended only through the first six arches on the side street. Joseph Urban designed its famed Marine Roof with maritime motifs, a place for dancing and fine dining; it also offered a magnificent view of New York. Having slipped into decline in modern times, the Bossert was bought by the Jehovah's Witnesses in 1984 and underwent extensive restoration. The image at publication is unchanged, although the bricks are white and a later canopy is smaller.

BROOKLYN EAGLE POST CARD, SERIES 75, No. 446.
THE MONTAGUE APARTMENT HOTEL, MONTAGUE ST.

◀ The Montague underwent an extensive rehabilitation through its 1981 conversion to co-operative residences. Later exterior preservation leaves the building at 105 Montague Street unchanged from its early appearance. The four-story building on its east lost its decorative details while the neighboring building, seen in a partial view with the Montague, remains well-preserved. The light is in the hall rather than the center of the Montague's entry ironwork.

◄ Organized in 1859, the Brooklyn Art Association dated from an era prior to commercial art dealing when artists held "receptions" to promote the sale of their paintings. They were able to erect this substantial Gothic Revival headquarters a decade later adjacent to the former Academy of Music at the left. The costly building, designed by Brooklyn's J. C. Cady and completed in 1870, also contained an art school. Caring for the building may have sapped the Association's vitality, as some functions, notably education, were absorbed by the Brooklyn Academy of Design. The building, once at 157 Montague Street, was pictured in Stiles' *Kings County Vol. 2.* The Association Building was remodeled as offices with a 1920s change of ownership, but succumbed at an unspecified date for the later office on the site now.

TRINITY CHURCH MONTAGUE & CLINTON STREETS, BROOKLYN, N. Y.

▲ Holy Trinity Protestant Episcopal Church, designed by Minard Lafever and built 1844-7 at the northwest corner of Montague and Clinton Streets, is seen looking west. It is pictured in the early postcard era, not long after its 175-foot spire, designed by Patrick C. Keely in 1866 and a highly-visible landmark, was removed in 1906. After Holy Trinity disbanded in 1957, the church was largely vacant until 1969, when St. Ann's relocated here from Livingston Street. An extensive restoration was undertaken by the parish, which is now known as St. Ann's and Holy Trinity Church and has been listed on the National Register since 1987. At the right is a partial view of George B. Post's 1881 Brooklyn Historical Society, formerly known as the Long Island Historical Society, which faces 128 Pierrepont Street.

Brooklyn Savings Bank, Clinton St., Brooklyn, N. Y.

▲ The Beaux-Arts headquarters of the Brooklyn Savings Bank, designed by Frank Freeman and built in 1893 at 141 Pierrepont Street on its northeast corner with Clinton Street, was long-esteemed as one of the business district's finest. However, after the bank, founded in 1827, built a high-rise across the street in the late 1950s, the old place became redundant to them and was acquired by the city. Preservationists had ardent hopes for saving the building, but little or no authority. The fine white granite building with a tile roof was razed in 1964, simultaneously with the Pennsylvania Station in New York, when the area was re-configured as part of the Cadman Plaza project. *Courtesy of Joan Kay.*

5 MINUTES TO MANHATTAN BY ANY SUBWAY

◄ The Hotel Touraine, designed by Frank S. Lowe for the Brooklyn Heights Improvement Company, was built around 1902 by the Thompson Starrett Company. The Touraine leased two- and three-room apartments, was home to the fine Palm Garden Restaurant, and attained a high level of elegance for apartment house living. The Crescent Athletic Club, adjacent on the right, maintained both downtown and waterfront clubhouses; the latter is pictured on page 95. These buildings at the northern stem of Clinton Street were taken down around the early 1960s for the Cadman Plaza project.

23 CLINTON STREET BROOKLYN, NEW YORK.

chapter three
Downtown Brooklyn

There are two hints that suggest that this image predates the card's c.1902 publication. The most visible is the absence of the cupola, built in 1898 to replace one destroyed by fire on February 26, 1895. In addition, while built as "City Hall" in pre-consolidation Brooklyn, the current name of Borough Hall was adopted in the years after 1898. The southwesterly view shows the northerly curve of Fulton Street and its elevated rail line. The latter's place in the foreground would be on the present Cadman Plaza East. The former County Courthouse is shown on its Joralemon site. The buildings on the left were demolished in 1955 for construction of the Supreme Court building.

Series 1321 A.

City Hall, Brooklyn, N. Y.

Davidson Brothers.

Designed by Gamaliel King, the Greek Revival Borough Hall at 209 Joralemon Street, between Cadman Plaza West and Court Street, was built between 1845-48. The 1898 replacement cupola was the design of Vincent C. Griffith and Stroughton and Stroughton. It is now topped by a figure of Justice, added in a renovation planned in 1980 and carried out over 1984-9. The government buildings around Borough Hall changed markedly well-prior to the 1950-60s Civic Center reconstruction. Note in the right background the character of Court Street south of the Temple Bar prior to 1920s office construction.

A new County Courthouse, also designed by Gamaliel King and dedicated in January 1859, was built on the site of the former Military Garden, "a place of resort famous in the village annals of Brooklyn," according to Stiles' *Brooklyn Volume 2*, and partially on the site of the Brooklyn Garden. After the county court was relocated from Flatbush to Brooklyn in 1825, a time when they were still separate municipalities, it is believed that it occupied a nearby building that was cleared when this one was erected. This image makes one suspect that the building was remodeled at some point.

COURT HOUSE, BROOKLYN, N. Y.

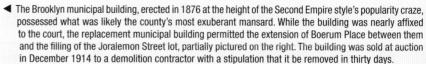

The Brooklyn municipal building, erected in 1876 at the height of the Second Empire style's popularity craze, possessed what was likely the county's most exuberant mansard. While the building was nearly affixed to the court, the replacement municipal building permitted the extension of Boerum Place between them and the filling of the Joralemon Street lot, partially pictured on the right. The building was sold at auction in December 1914 to a demolition contractor with a stipulation that it be removed in thirty days.

BROOKLYN EAGLE POST CARD, SERIES 42, No. 247.
MUNICIPAL BUILDING

▲ The cornerstone of the Hall of Records was laid on June 30, 1885, and the building was completed December 29, 1886, two days before due under contract. Prior to the 1904 expansion of the building, architects William Mundell and Rudolph L. Daus engaged in a public spitting contest because the former felt that he, the architect of the original building, should have had the commission, and the latter groused over the cement that had been used in the concrete. Interest dims after the destruction of the building and with the obscurity of information. However, there were other concerns — notably costs that curtailed the original expansion plan of a full fourth floor and a much-altered facade. A glimpse of the original building is in the first Borough Hall image while the piece of Temple Bar visible in the right background depicts the relationship of this building to nearby Court Street.

◄ The Brooklyn Municipal Building took many years to plan with a competition for designs announced at least as early as 1903. The new structure, designed by McKenzie, Voorhees, and Gmelin and completed in 1926, looms over Borough Hall on a late 1950s chrome. The latter was entered on the National Register of Historic Places in 1980. Boerum Place separates this building from the former Courthouse while the top of the Chamber of Commerce building is in the right background. Both tall structures can also be viewed in a sequence of the Court Street offices.

The underground connection with Manhattan was a post-consolidation transportation link that spurred Brooklyn's expansion in a manner comparable to the great Brooklyn Bridge. The Interborough Rapid Transit or the IRT, as it was known until numbered or lettered train route designations replaced original rail line names, opened in Manhattan in 1904, then tunneled under the East River, sending its first train to Brooklyn, on January 9, 1908. Brooklyn celebrated widely in recognition of the import to its prospective growth and well-being. The interesting underground view depicts tunnel construction and motive power, a third rail (under a protective cover) from which a "shoe" connected to the wheels draws electricity.

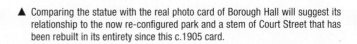

Beecher Monument, Court Sq., Brooklyn, N.Y.

▲ Comparing the statue with the real photo card of Borough Hall will suggest its relationship to the now re-configured park and a stem of Court Street that has been rebuilt in its entirety since this c.1905 card.

Beecher's statue, sculpted by John Quincy Adams Ward, is pictured at its prominent place in front of Borough Hall on its fine pedestal by Richard Morris Hunt, but like so many New York City monuments, it was moved and can be found a short distance away near Johnson Street. Beecher, a native of Connecticut, had an eight-year tenure at an Indianapolis church prior to his 1847 arrival at Plymouth (see page 19). He was a magnetic speaker, drawing great throngs to his orations. While it could be said his appeal to the fair sex was partially attributed to his support for women's suffrage, his looks and personality were the greater draws for their affection, which he returned, apparently at times too intimately. Theodore Tilton's 1874 suit claiming an adulterous relationship with his parishioner wife sought major damages. While Beecher won over the jury for an acquittal, he suffered in the court of public opinion. However, his enormous and enduring popularity kept him at Plymouth until his death. Note the original three-bay elevation of the Court Street façade of the Mechanics Bank Building.

▼ This view east from the bridge tower depicts the huge trolley station built to accommodate the rail traffic that had grown enormously since 1883. Note the long line of cars on the east-bound side. One searching for surviving landmarks will find the roof of the six-sided Long Island Safe Deposit Company and the edge of the Eagle Warehouse (see pages 17-18) in the lower right corner, the two separated by the Fulton Street elevated tracks. The church above them is no longer extant, as its lot is under the Brooklyn-Queens Expressway, but it was the Bethel Chapel, the first Brooklyn Heights home of the future Jehovah's Witnesses. It was bought by their founder on his arrival in New York, Pastor Charles Taze Russell, at a time when they were known as "the Russellites."

Brooklyn Bridge, New York. Brooklyn Approach

This c.1910 eastern view recedes into the shopping district, or the present Fulton Mall. Not only are the court and Hall of Records on the right gone, but the street was re-configured for the planning of the Civic Center. The former Telephone Building in the left background at the northeast corner of Willoughby and Lawrence Streets is the only prominent surviving landmark other than the Borough Hall cupola. The clock tower in the rear at Fulton and Nevins Streets is part of the former Fulton & Flatbush Storage Company, but only seven of its former seventeen stories survive. The card appears to have originated from a cropped photograph taken from Temple Bar.

The Mechanics Bank Building was ▶ erected in two sections. The original, which consists of three bays on the northwest corner of Court and Montague Streets, was designed by George L. Morse and completed in 1897. The extension, probably Morse's work as well, was added around 1905 at a time when Mechanics was absorbing other banks through merger. They, in turn, were merged into the Brooklyn Trust Company in 1931. The Brooklyn Dodgers maintained their offices here.

BROOKLYN EAGLE POST CARD, SERIES 34, NO. 204.
MECHANICS BANK BUILDING, COURT AND MONTAGUE STS.

The eight-story redbrick ▶ Garfield Building, designed by J. C. Cady & Co. and described by King as the "earliest of Brooklyn's great office buildings," is believed to have been completed in the early 1880s. Thus, one probably concludes it was named for the president who was assassinated in 1881. The tenant at grade was the Nassau National Bank, which was founded in 1859. The building was demolished in 1925 to make way for the 28-story office tower at 26 Court Street.

BROOKLYN EAGLE POST CARD, SERIES 22, NO. 131.
GARFIELD BUILDING, COURT AND REMSEN STREETS.

BROOKLYN EAGLE POST CARD, SERIES 25, NO. 148.
PHOENIX BUILDING, COURT STREET NEAR MONTAGUE.

◀ Architect E. L. Roberts is credited with the Second Empire style office built for the Phoenix Fire Insurance Company, according to his *Brooklyn Eagle* obituary of March 14, 1890. The building at 16 Court Street was replaced by the Court-Montague building pictured along the row in the nearby chrome card.

▲ The Court-Livingston at 66 Court Street, designed by Abraham J. Sinberg and completed around 1925 at the northwest corner of its namesake intersection, was in its early days known for its Chamber of Commerce tenant. Court-Livingston was converted to co-operative residences. The five buildings on the block south to Schermerhorn are largely intact, but the middle one appears to have been radically changed to accommodate a fast-food restaurant.

▲ The Temple Bar is the only survivor on this Court Street view looking south from the grounds in front of Borough Hall. In December 1884, the Dime Savings Bank moved from 367 Fulton Street to their new handsome marble Beaux-Arts headquarters located on the southwest corner of Remsen Street. This building, which was designed by Mercein Thomas, remained their headquarters until December 1908 when they moved to De Kalb Avenue. Plans had been announced to build an addition over the three-story building, but rising values on Court Street demanded greater remunerative utility of this prominent corner. Number 32 Court Street was completed here in 1918. The corner of Joralemon Street, visible on the left edge, was later filled by the extant 50 Court, or the Terminal Building, completed in 1914. Both of these structures are pictured in a companion image.

▲ Built in 1901 at 44 Court Street and named for the famed London landmark, George L. Morse's Beaux-Arts office Temple Bar stands as one of Brooklyn's endearing, even iconic business buildings. The Ionic columns at the entrance, pictured on a c.1910 card, are gone, replaced by dismal storefronts that mar the image at street level, but fortunately the three distinctive ogee-shaped cupolas survive intact.

BOROUGH HALL AND MUNICIPAL BLDG., BROOKLYN, N. Y.

The year of this white border card can be inferred as 1925. The evidence is provided by the new Municipal Building located behind Borough Hall, which was constructed that year, pictured along with a still-standing Garfield Building (minus it cupola) at the far right, which was demolished later in 1925. Adjacent to the left of the readily recognizable Temple Bar is the twelve-story Terminal Building, designed by William E. Lehman, at 50 Court which was completed in 1914. The 21-story 32 Court Street is to Temple Bar's right; it was designed by Starrett & VanVleck and completed in 1918.

2114 – Post Office, BROOKLYN, N.Y.

▲ The Romanesque post office at the northeast corner of Washington (left) and Johnson Streets, completed in 1892 and entered on the National Register in 1974, also housed the federal court. The post office has been removed, but the tower section of the building stands and is undergoing preservation in 2010.

Two of Brooklyn's tallest ▶ buildings were erected in the 1920s on Court Street. They are the Court-Remsen in the center, a 28-story tower designed by Schwartz & Gross and built in 1926 at number 26, and the Court-Montague adjacent on its right, forty stories, completed in 1927 at number 16 and designed by H. Craig Severance. The c.1959 chrome post-dates the New York State Supreme Court, pictured in partial view at the right.

▲ The grassy triangle in front of Borough Hall is now part of Columbus Park. The trees at right obscure the new Cadman Plaza West area, but the background provides two recognizable old structures: the tower of the old post office building, which is visible above the tent that enclosed its exterior for rehabilitation in 2010, and the Manhattan Bridge tower located further north at its left.

◄ The New York State Supreme Court at 360 Adams Street, which is a lower court in this state, was one of the earlier buildings erected on the S. Parkes Cadman Plaza civic improvement project that re-developed the Borough Hall-Court and Fulton Streets area. The building was completed in 1957, about a quarter-century after the Empire State Building, the best known commission of its architects, Shreve, Lamb, & Harrison.

▲ John Hill, proprietor of the Clarendon Hotel, recognized the importance of both postcards and the subway in building his trade. The Clarendon's location on the northwest corner of Washington and Johnson Streets, once part of the business area's street grid, was transformed by the 1950s construction of Cadman Plaza. The area is around the Korean War Veterans Plaza stem, where a narrow strip of park separates the east and west parts of Cadman Plaza.

New York's worst toll from an internal structure fire (thus, eliminating the *General Slocum* maritime and the September 11, 2001, terrorist disasters) was the Brooklyn Theatre blaze of December 5, 1876 (and not the often commemorated Triangle Shirtwaist fire of 1911). Over three hundred people were killed, most of them occupants of the cheap seats on the top floor where egress was hampered by a single, narrow staircase. Management was not acquitted well in the immediately following blame game, but it took years for now routine safety measures to be required. The theatre was located on Washington Street on a lot later occupied by the *Brooklyn Eagle* building, a spot now north of the New York Supreme Court Building. This image appeared on the cover of *Harper's Weekly*, December 23, 1876.

The Emma Stebbins (1815-1882) sculpture, carved possibly as early as 1861, like its Christopher Columbus subject, is much-traveled. The statue was claimed, although confirming details are lacking, to have been exhibited in two places in Manhattan. After it was rediscovered in 1934 at a Central Park maintenance yard, it was given a new home and installed that year on an Aymar Embury-designed base. The seven-foot tall, Italian marble figure was installed at its current position in front of the New York State Supreme Court on October 8, 1971, after the southern section of Cadman Plaza was renamed Columbus Park.

The huge Brooklyn World War II Memorial in Cadman Plaza was inspired by Robert Moses' wish to avoid many small and often inadequate memorials that occurred after World War I. This monument was a compromise after the winning design of a competition proved too costly to build. The pictured 25 by 100-foot granite panel is actually the south elevation of a two-story building designed by Stuart Constable and sculptor Elisabeth Gordon. The 24-foot high sculpted figures by the well-known artist Charles Keck are a male warrior with a sheathed sword and a woman and child, which symbolize love and family life. The dedication inscription honors the men and women of Brooklyn who fought for liberty in the Second World War.

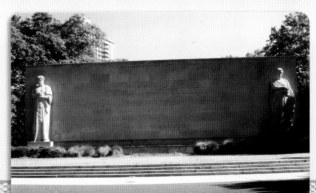

This bronze portrait and bas-relief, which honors Mayor William J. Gaynor, is the work of Adolph A. Weinman, then the sculptor-member of the Municipal Arts Commission. Unveiled May 12, 1926, at the Brooklyn end of the Manhattan Bridge, the piece was relocated to the northern end of Cadman Plaza in 1938. The inscription on the rear — "ours is a government of laws, not men" — reflects the mayor's pro-reform, anti-corruption ethic. Gaynor, born in 1851, became ill and died during his re-election campaign of 1913. Note that wound around the base is a chain of used Metrocards that were put together for use on June 11, 2010, for a student march across the Brooklyn Bridge to protest a proposed elimination of free rides for high school students.

▼ Fulton enjoyed a long run as downtown's most vibrant and prestigious shopping street. A key stem east of the Civic Center was transformed to Fulton Mall, a largely pedestrian strip that ostensibly bans private vehicles. This chrome card dates from around the year of that green 1953 Buick, an example that has only a front whitewall, an old tire decoration that one remembers if he ever had to clean them. Both Bickford's and Horn and Hardart are gone. The latter, which originated in Philadelphia, became a New York feeding, if not dining, landmark following their arrival in 1912. After the last closed in 1991, much of their simple fare became cherished as "comfort food." They are best remembered for their coin-operated, window-faced food racks where youngsters who carefully compared the sizes of sliced pie were amazed at their uniformity.

▲ The Roman Catholic Church on Long Island was founded on this site at the northeast corner of Jay and Chapel Streets in 1822. The church, now the St. James Catholic Basilica, has undergone major change from its origins as a modest structure. The edifice was expanded around 1844 by Patrick Charles Keely, but then was substantially destroyed by fire in 1889. Architect George H. Streeton designed the Georgian Revival reconstruction, completed in 1903, a structure little-changed in over a century. This 2010 image looks remarkably like the one on the *Brooklyn Eagle* postcard that was dropped for its inclusion. Following the establishment of the Diocese of Brooklyn in 1853, St. James was designated a "Pro-Cathedral" (provisional) in anticipation of its replacement. A new cathedral was begun, but not completed and is pictured on page 44. The bronze plaques beside the center door signifies a change in the church's status, as it was designated a minor basilica in 1952 (left), and commemorates the October 3, 1979, visit of Pope John Paul II.

Founded in 1909, Joe's claim to fame could stem from the great ▶ number of postcards it gave away, enough to make this finely-colored linen example still common. The contrast of the red and greens is as charming as is the one-time ability to walk on Fulton Street before it became congested. Or, perhaps Joe's had an army of followers since they claimed to be able to seat 1,000 diners. The building was demolished in the early 1960s when the lot was needed for a street re-configuration for the emerging Civic Center.

Brooklyn's Famous Eating Place

JOE'S RESTAURANT • 326-334 Fulton Street, Brooklyn, New York

Shopping district, Fulton St., Brooklyn, N. Y.

Fulton Street — Heart of the Shopping District, Brooklyn, N. Y.

▲ This Fulton Street view, west from Bond Street, is still distinguished by the handsome Renaissance Revival store and office at number 505 on the right. When one looks over the large, loud contemporary storefronts that appear to scream at the viewer, he can still be rewarded by spotting gems on this busy stem, such as the intact bell tower at the left on the west side of Hoyt Street. *Courtesy of Moe Cuocci.*

▲ An "OC Co." medallion in the cornice crest still revealed in 2010 that Oppenheim Collins was the former tenant at the northeast corner of Lawrence Street, although their name over the door was by then covered. The view east on this c.1940s linen shows a block that is largely intact, but, oh how the famed names that made Fulton a major shopping thoroughfare are long since gone. Namms, Loeser, and Martin are among the fading memories and even Abraham & Straus, behind the shadows on the south side of the street, had to be reincarnated by its corporate owners as the better-recognized Macy's, despite the failure of the latter in its previous incarnation.

Todd Williams' wall painting at number 240 made a drab stem of ▶ Livingston Street colorful for a spell. It is pictured over a Bohack, a once-popular representative of the Brooklyn supermarket scene. The structures of the Livingston streetscape, looking west in 1970, are intact. However, the Williams' painting, intended as temporary art for City Walls, Inc., has long since been covered and a Goodwill store replaced the Bohack. The nearest intersection is Elm Place, at the right by the six-story building, while the Court-Livingston building is discernible in the distance.

Head–Quarters of Fire Department. Brooklyn, N. Y. July 14 /05

No. 710   Published by The American News Company, New York-Leipzig-Berlin

The New York City Transit Museum, at their 370 Jay Street headquarters, has a multi-level exhibition space that features changing historic displays. Its highlight, though, is its visitor access on rolling stock that sits on the rails of an abandoned station. This example is a 1903 B.M.T. "Q" car, an "all wood elevated open-end gate car." It was rebuilt in 1938 for the World's Fair, with closed ends and side doors, and restored in 1969.

▼ Look, it is incredulous that cars and buses could not only coexist, but also could even make left turns at one of downtown's busiest intersections! Note their crossing over the redundant trolley tracks. This c.1940 linen lacks clarity, the long-time rap against this type of card. It does, however, enable essentials of the streetscape to be discerned; notably the building on the southwest corner at left, which retains its integrity, and the place opposite with its flat, bare angled wall. A metal and glass structure is on the northeast corner in 2010 while off the center the dome of the Dime Savings Bank (right) and the office towers of Court Street (left) can be spotted.

B22:—FULTON STREET LOOKING WEST FROM JUNCTION OF FLATBUSH AVE. AND FULTON ST.

BROOKLYN, N. Y.   48697

▲ Frank Freeman designed the Richardsonian Romanesque Brooklyn Fire Department Headquarters, completed in 1884, when Brooklyn was still an independent city. While that status is depicted on this c.1905 card, managerial authority was transferred to New York after the cities consolidated in 1898. The building still draws attention to its nineteenth century origins in relatively well-preserved condition despite the loss of some terra-cotta decoration. It stands on a block now dominated by a new Metrotech structure on the north (left) and a later low-rise business building on the south. The fire department's headquarters, which was entered on the National Register of Historic Places in 1972, was converted to apartment use in 1989.

LOUNGE, BROOKLYN ROSELAND, FULTON AT FLATBUSH AVE., BROOKLYN, N. Y.

◀ Puffery marked the dance hall's advertising message printed on the back: "Dance in a palace of beauty – Indescribably different is Roseland." They also claimed that in the turmoil and whirlpool of Brooklyn's existence, "It is still called romance." The card's contribution to this book is to show that the cool colors of red and black could also be appealingly printed on a linen.

▼ Erected around 1890, the Renaissance Revival Bijou Theatre at Smith and Livingston Streets has an atypical corner location. Later, mid-block became the predominate sites for theatres, as they were typically built with a small entrance that led to the building's large-volume box behind it. The building came down at an unspecified date at a much-changed intersection. *Courtesy of Joan Kay.*

▲ The new New Montauk Theatre, erected in 1895 at Fulton and DeKalb, replaced both an earlier New Montauk, which was reportedly moved and renamed in response to a re-configuration of Flatbush Avenue, and an earlier Montauk Theatre on Fulton Street. The Elks led the cornerstone laying on April 20, 1895, and the house, containing an 85 by 100-foot auditorium that seated 1,750, opened September 16 when the Marie Tavary Opera Company performed *Verdi's Il Trovatore.* The place was razed in 1925 for the construction of a business building. *Courtesy of Joan Kay.*

▲ The twelve-story Fox Theatre was designed by C. Howard Crane and Kennett Franzheim to be one of the nation's finest. Completed in 1928, the building, with offices above grade, featured a 55-foot high grand lobby, an auditorium that seated 4,000, a specially designed pipe organ, and rich marble halls and foyers. William Fox's Fox Theatres Corp. took a thirty-year lease on the building, which filled most of the well-sited, triangular block of Flatbush Avenue, left, Fulton Street, right, and Nevins Street. The Fox opened August 31, 1928, with a showing of *Street Angel.* Alas, the Fox's days of glory had a relatively short run, doomed as a consequence of a 1950s decline in movie attendance and the area's fraying at the edges in the 1960s. Both took a toll, resulting in the Fox's closing in November 1970. The building was demolished early the next year and was replaced by a modern office building.

37

Board of Health Building, Brooklyn, New York.

SYNAGOGUE BETH ELOHIM, STATE STREET, NEAR HOYT.

▲ The Board of Health planned an elaborate state-of-the-art facility when they built their new headquarters in 1910 to cover the block at 295 Flatbush Avenue Extension, its northeast corner with Willoughby Street. The five-story white marble building, designed by James Gamble Rogers, contained a clinic, laboratory, and special entrances for children with school certification needs and walk-ins. It included an isolation ward in the basement, disinfecting rooms, as well as records vaults, offices, and lecture rooms. The handsome Classical Revival building hardly lasted to attain landmark stature. If tempted to think that destroying useful, appealing structures and basing local decisions on the availability of federal funds is a recent phenomenon, consider that this fine building, which was less than three decades old, was razed around 1938 because it did not take full advantage of its plot and Works Progress Administration funds were available for the replacement structure now on the site.

▲ Founded in 1861, the Congregation Beth Elohim was the third oldest Brooklyn Jewish synagogue. They moved from Boerum Hill a few years after this c.1905 card to Eighth Avenue and Garfield Place in Park Slope. By 1914 they were listed as the third largest congregation in Brooklyn with 425 contributing members.

◄ St. Agnes Roman Catholic Church, the most imposing and the largest structure in Carroll Gardens and surrounding neighborhoods, links the practices of Patrick C. Keely, who designed their first church, and his son-in-law Thomas F. Houghton. Completed in 1905, this Gothic edifice at 417 Sackett Street, its northeast corner with Hoyt Avenue, rebuilt a church that was destroyed by fire on July 2, 1901. The parish, founded in 1875, initially worshipped in a small, frame church at Hoyt and DeGraw Streets, which was replaced in 1882 by a 172-foot long Gothic stone church. Houghton, a parishioner, designed the latter.

◀ The Richardsonian Romanesque Germania Club, designed by Frank Freeman and built in 1890 at 120 Schermerhorn Street, was not only one of the city's most ornate, but also the headquarters for one of its most exclusive social and influential business circles. The building, which filled most of its 70 by 100-foot plot, contained a twenty-foot square interior lot and a fourth floor containing a fully-equipped theatre that could seat 1,000 in a space that also doubled as a ballroom. Ignore the card's incorrect label. A publisher of a long run of five hundred cards, the *Brooklyn Eagle* is entitled to an infrequent mistake, as the wary viewer knows that postcards from any source are prone to error. A mislabeled card is the least of the indignities Freeman suffered. This building was destroyed in the 1920s for construction of a subway that ran underneath Schermerhorn. Other losses of his oeuvre include the nearby Thomas Jefferson Association Building, the actual Democratic headquarters, and the Bushwick Democratic Clubhouse, neither of which are herein, but also the Hotel Margaret and Brooklyn Savings Bank, which are pictured on pages 21 and 24 respectively.

◀ The Gowanus Canal was begun around 1849 by Edwin C. Litchfield, who expanded a creek that followed the same 5,700-foot course from Hamilton Avenue to Douglass Street. The 100-foot wide canal, which was planned to facilitate industrial growth in the surrounding area, was an unqualified success on that count. For years it was an active waterway. However, in its time, factories on bodies of water too often found them a convenient place to pour waste; as a result, the Gowanus Canal became a dump. It was in a foul state since at least the end of the nineteenth century, but one might hardly notice that quality on this *Eagle* card depicting a tranquil vista looking east. Clean-up had been well-underway for years when the waterway received heightened public awareness by its designation as a Superfund site in 2010.

The development of high-rise condominiums around the Flatbush Avenue Extension, north of Fulton and east of Metro Tech, reflects the significant improvement of an area that had languished in its long-term dismal state until the recent past. Metro Tech has brought Myrtle Avenue, once depressed by the elevated rail line, to life. In addition, the recent renascence of the Fort Greene neighborhood is spreading westward. The Toren, a Skidmore, Owings, & Merrill aluminum and glass 38-story, 399-foot tower, at 150 Myrtle Avenue, had been hailed prior to construction for its extensive "green" environmental features and again after it was built for its outstanding aesthetic appeal. ▶

▲ The Independent Subway Bridge on the F line is one of New York's great but under-appreciated structures. One can ride over it for years without realizing how the soaring steel and concrete structure dominates the landscape around the Gowanus Canal. It was built to go over the canal because the grounds around it were not conducive to a tunnel and elevated to its lofty height to observe older navigation clearance rules that had become excessive. The view, south of Smith Street and east of Hamilton Avenue, pictures the structure with wrapping affixed as part of a preservation project, in a perspective that has long been a favorite of artists.

Northern Brooklyn

This section has the book's most diverse make-up and even an idiosyncratic territorial definition. It includes Williamsburg and Greenpoint, which are linked historically and in contemporary planning, with Fort Greene and Clinton Hill, which are also often viewed together, but not with the aforementioned two neighborhoods. A one-time agrarian Williamsburg was remade by its namesake bridge, which provided a path for striving Manhattan Lower East Side Jews to find new home in then uncongested Brooklyn. Greenpoint, linked with Williamsburg historically as part of the town of Bushwick, developed industry, including maritime trades along its waterfront. Both sections are enjoying growth and new development into the early twenty-first century through both gentrification and new settlement from traditional ethnics, including Jews in Williamsburg and Poles in Greenpoint. New zoning, the need to preserve elements of the past and the aspirations of those who improved the areas not to be driven out by rising rents characterize the current scene here.

Fort Greene and Clinton Hill are two of Brooklyn's great success stories. While both in the latter twentieth century were riddled with the usual urban ills and the crime that accompanies them, gentrification has increased desirability, raised prices and brought a new residential mix. Clinton Hill's enhancement was a return to past glory as during the end of the nineteenth century, the Hill, which did not need "Clinton" for the speaker to be understood, was among the city's most prestigious districts.

chapter four
Fort Greene

The Williamsburgh Savings Bank tower will remain the historic name of the 512-foot former office long after the passing of that once-venerable thrift institution. The Romanesque-influenced building, Brooklyn's tallest, was designed by Halsey, McCormack, & Helmer and completed in 1929 at 1 Hanson Place, its northeast corner with Ashland Place. The 27-foot diameter clock was for many years the country's largest four-face timepiece. The domed top, representing a symbol of Brooklyn, was chosen as the borough's contribution to the New York Mets' logo. The Williamsburgh used to give away ceramic banks as new account premiums. One wonders if examples can be found in the weekly flea markets held in the ornate former banking lobby.

Long Island R. R. Station, Brooklyn, N. Y.

◄ This station, designed by the obscure H. F. Saxcelbey, or maybe Saxelby, was completed in 1906, a successor to an 1877 Long Island Railroad Atlantic Avenue terminal. It, in turn, was demolished around 1988 to be replaced by a retail entrance to the train, the Atlantic Terminal Mall. The terminal anchored Times Plaza, a five-street juncture formed by three major thoroughfares — Atlantic, Flatbush, and Fourth Avenues — and two side streets, Ashland and Hanson Places; it was named for the defunct *Brooklyn Daily Times*, which published nearby.

This c.1940 view, east of Hanson Place, ► suggests why many linen cards are disdained: it lacks clarity. This card is also absent the vivid colors that redeem popular examples of the genre. The streetscape provides a partial view of the entrance at left to the Williamsburgh Savings Bank's opulent banking room, the Long Island Railroad Terminal at right, and the YMCA. Adjacent to the bank is Hanson Place Central United Methodist Church on the northwest corner of St. Felix Street, which was completed in 1931. The tall white apartment building is 62 Hanson Place; in 1930 it was raised from six to twelve stories on a steel frame engineered to accommodate anticipated later additions.

B13:— HANSON PLACE SHOWING L.I. R.R. DEPOT AND Y.M.C.A. BUILDING, BROOKLYN, N. Y.

▲ A $500,000 gift from the widowed Mrs. William Van Rennselear Smith spurred the erection of the Central Branch Young Men's Christian Association at 55 Hanson Place as a memorial to their son, YMCA activist Clarence E. Smith. The building, said to have been the largest and costliest YMCA in the world, was designed by Trowbridge & Ackerman and completed in 1915. It attained numerous superlatives for size and facilities. After significant service as a residence for men, later incarnations included a center for drug addicts in the 1970s, a homeless shelter in the 1980s, and state offices by the 1990s, its present occupancy after a major renovation. Airplanes were at times inserted on postcards to capture the emerging interest in travel by flight. They were typically small, crude additions, but this sketch captures the spirit of aviation and makes the plane and its beam a co-focal point on a card published by the Y.

◀ The Brooklyn Academy of Music is shown at 30 Lafayette Avenue. Erected in 1908, this Renaissance Revival concert hall was designed by Herts & Tallant on a block running from St. Felix Street, left, to Ashland Place. The organization, established in 1859, felt the new hall would invigorate the borough's cultural life, which prophetically was believed to have been slipping behind Manhattan's following the 1898 consolidation of the city. The stamp was placed on the face of this c.1909 Valentine & Sons card in the style of some European usage.

A long-struggling Academy, following purchase ▶ by the city in 1951, was turned over to the Brooklyn Institute of Arts and Sciences for operation. This chrome card from later that decade reflects the modernization of the period. Universally known by its acronym BAM, the house has enjoyed a remarkable renascence and has regained stature as a major venue in Brooklyn cultural life. It was entered on the National Register of Historic Places in 2006.

▲ The same view on a 1950s chrome, which substitutes a 1952 Buick for the horse and carriage on the older card, has a new canopy and posters recalling two of the period's operatic stars. Absent, however, are the balustrades and the cornice, removed during 1953 repairs, which made the building for many years resemble the author after a trip to the barber. However, their recent replacement has made the building intact once more. Note the Williamsburgh Savings Bank building in the background.

◀ Fort Greene Park occupies a rectangular three hundred-acre plot bordered by Myrtle and De Kalb Avenues on the north and south and St. Edwards and Washington Park Streets on the west and east. The latter is the park's original name. The park was renamed for its Fort Greene neighborhood, an area that honors Revolutionary War general Nathaniel Greene. Frederick Law Olmsted and Calvert Vaux designed the park in the 1860s, which was built on an elevation with a fine view of New York. The area was fortified during the Revolution when it was known as Fort Putnam. The field pieces date from the Mexican War.

Bishop John Loughlin acquired the block founded by Greene, Vanderbilt, Lafayette, and Clermont Avenues ▶ in order to plan a grand cathedral to be named Immaculate Conception. He laid the cornerstone on June 21, 1868, for the massive French Gothic church, designed by Patrick C. Keely, who took inspiration from the cathedral at Rouen. The building rose from the ground about twelve feet and became partially utilized in 1878 when the Chapel of St. John was completed in one corner. That richly designed space hinted at the prospective grandeur of what would have been the largest church in America. It was not to be. The project languished in its incomplete state after the bishop's attentions and finances were directed to social welfare concerns. Completing the cathedral was reconsidered after Keely's death when English architect John Francis Bentley, who designed the Catholic Westminster Cathedral in London, was hired to update the plans. However, they, too, were incomplete at Bentley's death. The ill-fated project eventually died and, after the beginnings of this grand project were razed in 1931, even its memory faded.

The cathedral would have ▶ represented Keely's chef d'oeuvre and cemented and elevated his historical reputation, which suffers, in part, from an enormous output, upwards of seven hundred churches and buildings for churches, of which only a minority has been identified. Much of his early work was for new parishes, which grew and replaced those first churches, at times by Keely, although with a scant historical record. Bishop John Loughlin (1817-1891) was a modest man with simple tastes who lived most

of his bishopric in the old, inelegant rectory. He oversaw construction of this new residence that was designed by Keely and built in 1887 at 367 Clermont Avenue, but he confined himself in his last years to one small space. Its mix of styles includes a mansard roof, a nod to a motif in many Keely-designed rectories, but in this instance utilized well-after the Second Empire style's fall from fashion. The residence, a handsome, solid building fitting for its purpose and occupied for many years as the diocesan chancery, is now a residence attached to Bishop Loughlin Memorial High School (seen at the right).

Monument and Steps, Fort Green Park, Brooklyn, N.Y.

◀ After the remains of Revolutionary War captives who died in the Wallabout Bay prison ships were discovered during Brooklyn Navy Yard excavations the previous winter and given a military funeral ceremony at Plymouth Church on June 16, 1900, they were carried in a procession to Fort Greene Park for burial. A temporary memorial was built. Stanford White designed this 148-foot Doric column, the world's tallest, on which was surmounted a tripod for a memorial flame sculpted by Adolph A. Weinman. The remains were removed from their old vault for placement at this new monument in September 1908 prior to the shaft's dedication that November 14th with a major ceremony in which a large crowd was joined by the governors of New York, New Jersey, and Delaware.

PRATT INSTITUTE, BROOKLYN, N.Y.

Pratt Institute occupies the Clinton Hill tract bordered by Willoughy to DeKalb Avenues and Classon Avenue to Hall Street — streets that were cut-off to form an urban campus containing structures from its 1887 founding by industrialist Charles Pratt, along with later expansion. The beginnings of this acclaimed fine arts college also embraced industrial and domestic arts, as well as technology. By 1905, it claimed 3,500 students and 124 instructors. The Main Building in the center, built 1885-7, was designed by Lamb and Rich and extensively restored in the late 1990s. The Domestic Arts Building is to its right, while The Thrift, at the left, was established to promote Pratt's belief that saving by students should be encouraged. The latter was razed for the 1926-7 construction of Memorial Hall.

The Mohawk, Washington and Greene Aves., Brooklyn, N.Y.

The Pratt power plant in the 1887 East Building, originally the Machine Shop Building, includes three electrically-powered Ames Iron Works steam generators that were installed in 1900 and still supply 120-volt direct current electrical service to part of the campus. The American Society of Mechanical Engineers has designated the facility a Historical Mechanical Engineering Landmark while the Pratt region has been a National Register Historic District since 2005. The image is a c.1960s chrome.

The outstanding residences on this block of Clinton Avenue, now part of Fort Greene, is reminiscent of old Clinton Hill when it was a center of late nineteenth century residential opulence. Then simply known as "The Hill," architects erected high-design mansions for the city's affluent who were moving east to the hill and south to Park Slope from their traditional Brooklyn Heights enclave. Clinton Avenue, a century after it was pictured on this soft-color view from H. Hagemeister, a publisher of outstanding urban scene cards, can be an adventure for the street explorer in tracing the change of its built environment — notably its mix of surviving mansions and apartment houses that were built in the first four decades of the twentieth century.

Clinton Ave., Brooklyn, N.Y.

The Mohawk at 379 Washington Avenue, between Greene and Lafayette Avenues, was designed by Neville & Bagge, a firm that had an enormous body of apartment house work. When completed in 1904, the Mohawk entered the market as a luxury rental. As apartment living was still considered novel to some in the more respectable classes, this Beaux-Arts example offered a first-floor general dining room as an amenity. The Mohawk suffered a decline over the decades and reached its nadir as a down-on-its-heels hotel in the late twentieth century. However, a fine restoration has returned the place to apartment occupancy, a change that reflects the rising fortunes of a renascent Fort Greene and Clinton Hill.

The need of Brooklyn's numerous lodges for a common meeting place ▶ inspired the 1906-9 construction of the Brooklyn Masonic Temple at 317 Clermont Avenue, its northwest corner with Lafayette Avenue. Two firms, Lord & Hewlett and Pell & Corbett, designed the Classical Revival, approximately one hundred feet square marble temple finished with colored glazed terra-cotta. Double and triple height lodge rooms and an auditorium seating 1,000 were shared by thirty-five lodges in 1912. Under management of the Brooklyn Masonic Guild, a 1914 advertisement offered to the public, "Superior entertainment, lectures, musicales, amateur theatricals, fairs, falls and dancing parties, moving pictures, mass meetings, and all social functions." At publication, the temple remains available for public use.

Masonic Temple, Brooklyn, N.Y.

▲ The c.1910 real photo card of the Home for the Aged on Clinton Avenue is a gripping image that merits inclusion even absent details. One suspects this fine Second Empire style building was originally a house that was expanded compatible with its original construction prior to the addition in the rear. *Courtesy of Joan Kay.*

▲ Established locally in 1855, the Sisters of Mercy built this convent that opened in 1862 at 273 Willoughby Avenue. Its beginning was the central section of a now U-shaped building, to which were added large wings on the west and east in 1883 and 1892 respectively. The facility, which was more than a home for the nuns, as it housed a residence for needful girls between the ages of two and eighteen, now fills the north side of the block between Classon Avenue and Taffee Place. Occupancy has been reduced to a few resident sisters while the building suffers from deferred maintenance. Its residential function suggests the possibility for adaptive use, but its condition may force the building to be removed. The place is a major preservation concern at publication.

Adelphi Academy, founded in 1863 by the elder Charles Pratt and incorporated six years later, ▶ was an early success and soon attained stature for excellence. They expanded throughout their early decades around Clifton and St. James Places and Lafayette Avenue, where they built a number of Romanesque buildings. The founder's son, also Charles, paid for a new building in 1888; this Romanesque structure, designed by Charles C. Haight, faces Clifton Place. After Adelphi moved to Garden City, Long Island, in 1925, their Brooklyn complex was incorporated into Pratt Institute.

Adelphi Institute, Brooklyn, N.Y.

General Slocum Monument, Brooklyn, N.Y.

◀ General Henry Warner Slocum, born in 1827 in Onondaga County, New York, served as a commander in the Civil War, where he saw extensive battlefield action, and was later elected to the House of Representatives. He was memorialized in 1905 by this equestrian statue sculpted by Frederick William MacMonnies, which is mounted on a pedestal designed by Stanford White. Decorative features include an eagle in relief and two medallions on each side. It is pictured c.1910 at its original Eastern Parkway and Bedford Avenue location. The figure was moved, either during subway construction or for traffic control reasons, as have many of the city's large, heroic monuments, to the Bartel-Pritchard Square entrance to Prospect Park and later to its present location, the Grand Army Plaza (see page 64). Slocum, who died in Brooklyn in 1894, is the namesake of the steamship *General Slocum*, infamous in maritime annals for the on-board fire in 1904 that took a toll of over 1,000 lives.

Brooklyn College, BROOKLYN, N.Y.

The original Brooklyn College, a Jesuit institution that opened in September 1908 at 1150 Carroll Street at ▶ Nostrand Avenue, should not be confused with the public school dating from two decades later. Its upper level instructional program offered Bachelor of Arts degrees while its "classical high school" department prepared students for college. This Brooklyn College never secured a firm financial footing and was forced to close in 1921. The card is contemporary with the school's opening when about two hundred students enrolled in a building for which later expansion was anticipated. Indeed, a May 1912 announcement (*Times*, May 4th) indicated that a 700-foot long building (designed by Raymond F. Almirall) for Jesuit instruction, which, one is tempted to infer, was to be an extension of this, was planned. The structure is readily recognizable in its present incarnation as Medgar Evers College.

◀ The Swedish Hospital, which incorporated in July 1896, opened their hospital at Sterling Place and Rogers Avenue, apparently starting with this Second Empire style house. The place's dedication and "opening" on June 24, 1906, was reported by the *Times* the next day; it referenced the "…large brick building, which has been remodeled to suit the purposes of the hospital. To this a two-story brick annex has been built." They were able to accommodate sixty patients, who could be treated in the Swedish language. This Rotograph card, posted in 1908, pre-dates the expansion. An image of the dedication and annex are pictured on a *Brooklyn Eagle* card not shown herein.

St. Mary's Hospital, Brooklyn, N.Y.

▲ Time-travelers searching for the view north on Classon Avenue from Quincy Street, pictured here on a c.1910 real photo card, would recognize the scene from the two corner buildings. The west side building on the left even retains its cornice while the east side retains most of its integrity, the absence of its cornice notwithstanding. *Courtesy of Joan Kay.*

▲ Bishop Loughlin laid the cornerstone for St. Mary's Hospital in October 1879 and then returned for the formal opening on December 17, 1882. At the time, the building had a frontage of 229 feet on St. Marks Avenue and extended back 165 feet on Rochester Avenue. Operated by the Sisters of Charity, expansions of this facility were anticipated at the outset and in time would fill the block to Buffalo Avenue. This c.1910 card puzzles the careful viewer and makes one suspect that it combines the finished building at right with renderings for additions. However, prior to 1910, the later construction had been published showing a roof and windows compatible with the original. Remodeling does not seem to have been likely, so this card is a mystery. St. Mary's was a non-sectarian health center that served the local community into the twenty-first century. However, it closed in March 2005 and was later demolished. *Courtesy of Joan Kay.*

L. J. Storage Warehouse, Brooklyn, N.Y.

◄ The Long Island Storage Warehouse built this handsome Italian Renaissance Revival warehouse c.1900 on the southwest corner of Nostrand (left) and Gates Avenues. The striking classical doorways not only seem more suitable to a bank, but also mark the entrances to the Jenkins Trust Company. This tenant is pictured on a *Brooklyn Eagle* card that can lead one to infer that Jenkins was the building's owner. Its occupants changed over the years, first when Jenkins became Lafayette Trust in 1908 and later, when in 1944, Empire State Warehouses bought the building, which is still-standing and instantly recognizable at publication.

Charles Cooper built this distinctive Commercial ► Italianate business building around 1887, located on the southeast corner of Fulton Street (the shorter end on the left) and Bedford Avenue. At the same time, Cooper also built four 20 by 60 feet stores and dwellings on the Fulton Street side where a glimpse of one is visible. His architect was Frank Keith Irving. The Cooper Building was lost at an unspecified time; a one-story store occupies the lot now.

The Brooklyn Trust Company (Bedford Branch)

The c.1910 real photo card of the Church of the Nativity and its school ▶
on Madison Street at the corner of Classon Avenue (right) reflects
the rise and fall of the Catholic church in the Bedford-Stuyvesant
neighborhood. The interior of the Gothic church, which was designed
by Thomas Houghton and completed in 1873, was transformed from
plainness and severity "to one of the most beautiful houses of worship
in the City of Churches," according to a report in the *Times* on May 28,
1893. This edition announced that day's blessing of a new, massive,
white marble altar that had been designed by Raymond F. Almirall, an
architect and parishioner who was then studying in Paris. Almirall later
designed for Nativity an Italianate-style church that was built in 1916
on the pictured corner. After Nativity was absorbed into the St. Peter
Claver parish in 1973, this church was sold to another congregation.
Courtesy of Joan Kay.

◀ The Labor Lyceum, which was founded
by the Central Labor Organization
of New York in 1882 as a gathering
place for social, personal, cultural, and
educational improvement and related
gatherings for the working man, was
destroyed by fire in December 1900.
The cornerstone for its replacement
was laid on May 30, 1902, at 949
Willoughby Avenue, a new location
a short distance from the destroyed
building. While it is unknown when
the labor functions ended, the building
remains remarkably unchanged,
apparently now in residential use.
Courtesy of Joan Kay.

The handsome Renaissance ▶
Revival Fulton Theatre, which
stood on Fulton Street near
Bedford Avenue, appears to date
c.1900. Its name was beamed
to a wide audience on the
water tank, a type of structure
inimitably characteristic of the
New York City skyline. Note
the tower's advertisement of
the theatrical staple of the
era, vaudeville. The theatre
appears not to have survived.
Courtesy of Joan Kay.

Grant Monument, Bedford Ave., Brooklyn, N.Y. Feb. 22 90-
E. S. S.

▲ The William Ordway Partridge equestrian statue of Ulysses S. Grant was presented by the Union League Club to the city at an April 25, 1896, ceremony at the Dean Street-Bedford Avenue intersection, thereafter known as Grant Square. Grant's namesake grandson was present to unveil the fifteen feet, eight-inch figure, which stands on a sixteen-foot pedestal, while Governor Morton reviewed the following parade. It is still there, making its run of 115 years in its original location a probable city record for a large statue located amidst heavy traffic. Its durability there is aided by a small traffic island.

GRANT SQUARE, BROOKLYN, N.Y.

Union League Club, Brooklyn, N.Y.

C. M. A. 1911.

◀ Consider the turn-of-the-twentieth century prestige, even elegance, of Bedford, a section now universally hyphenated with adjacent Stuyvesant, when Bedford claimed such structures as one of the city's most impressive equestrian statues, President Ulysses S. Grant, who still stands at his namesake square where Rogers Avenue branches southwest from Bedford Avenue at Dean and Bergen Streets. At the right was one of Brooklyn's most exclusive social organizations, the Union League Club, while on the left is a glimpse of one of Brooklyn's imposing armories. In their day, armories were a significant enhancement of their local street environments. This example was built for the 23rd Regiment. Louis Seitz hired Montrose W. Morris to design three artistic apartment buildings for the area. One, the particularly striking Imperial, is visible in the center background while the Alhambra is pictured near this image.

▲
◀ Although the Union League Club claimed to be a social organization, its members were so ardent in their advocacy of Republicanism that it was, for practical purposes, a political club as well; that status is suggested by the terra cotta heads of Lincoln and Grant on the facade. Their architect, Peter J. Lauritzen, chosen after selection in a blind competition, designed a well-appointed and decorated Romanesque building. Completed in 1890, it extends ninety-six feet on its Bedford Avenue façade while fronting fifty feet on Dean Street. The interior was filled with the usual dining, entertaining, recreational, and sleeping facilities. The tower, a nod to the then-popular Queen Anne style, seems out of place. Compare the book with the contemporary scene: the former clubhouse still stands, absent the tower, and is now occupied by the Grant Square Senior Citizen Center.

▲ The Alhambra, a Montrose W. Morris design for developer Louis Seitz, was described by the *Brooklyn Eagle,* as it neared completion in 1890, as the largest and most luxurious apartment house in the city. The five-story Romanesque residence at 500-518 Nostrand Avenue, which ran the full block from Macon (left) to Halsey Streets, incorporated a variety of masonry and colors beginning with Connecticut brownstone at the base. Lake Superior red sandstone marked the first floor while light salmon pink Columbus pressed brick and red terra-cotta were above. The six apartments each had eight or ten rooms and each floor contained open fireplaces and parlors that were formed into one of the several towers. The building declined in modern times, incurred extensive fire damage, but the Alhambra was extensively restored in 1998.

▼ J. J. Hart's mid-twentieth century linen advertising card for his Ford dealership emphasized trucks, reflective of the then-industrialized surroundings of his 1095 Atlantic Avenue location. The area, between Bedford and Franklin Avenues is hardly recognizable six decades later. *Courtesy of the late Gary Dubnik.*

▲ The cornerstone of St. John the Baptist Church was laid on his feast day, June 24, in 1888. The Patrick C. Keely design for the 204-foot long by 85-foot wide edifice, well-sited on Willoughby Avenue between Stuyvesant and Lewis Avenues, was to result in one of the most costly and imposing houses of worship in the city. Its Romanesque style was a departure from the architect's usual Gothic while the church's ample budget enabled Keely to demonstrate capabilities for an expansive structure, as compared to the tight cost constraints he worked under for much of his career. St. John's was one of Keely's last churches. He suffered a stroke and was an invalid during the last six years of his life. He died in 1896.

The arches and columns of the transept still suggest ▶ the grandeur of St. John's, as does its stained glass and statuary. However, the challenges of keeping churches with diminishing congregations resulted in the reduction of interior space by cutting off the front and rear of the interior and hanging a lower ceiling. The fiscal challenges of maintaining urban Catholic schools have resulted in many closures, including St. John's in 2010. Pictured is their last eighth grade graduation on June 18, 2010.

Atlantic Avenue Station. EAST NEW YORK

▲ The Fulton Elevated crossed the Long Island Railroad at the key Van Sinderen Avenue juncture, where a number of lines met within this East New York block. *Courtesy of Joan Kay.*

BROOKLYN EAGLE POST CARD, SERIES 44. No. 261.
HOUSE OF THE GOOD SHEPHERD

▲ The Sisters of the Good Shepherd, which traces its origins to a religious community formed in France in 1641, are guided in their later reorganization by the philosophy of St. Mary Euphrasia, who, in 1835, established a new worldwide community based on the conviction that "one person is of more value than a world." Their Brooklyn house, founded in 1868, built this Second Empire convent, completed at Hopkinson Avenue and Pacific Street, around 1875. Their mission contemporary with the c.1905 card was "shelter and reformation of erring girls and women," according to King, but their modern mission is to provide care, education, and opportunity to needful girls. This complex was acquired by the City and demolished for low-income housing at an unknown date, perhaps in the 1960s.

BROOKLYN NAVY YARD ENTRANCE

▲ The Brooklyn Navy Yard traces its origins to the United States Navy's 1801 purchase of a Wallabout Bay tract. Once activity commenced after a few years, the yard built and repaired vessels of every description for over a century and a half, a record that can and has filled a book. Late nineteenth century growth of the Navy Yard justified, and in today's security terms, probably required, a new entrance, which was begun in June 1895 by P. J. Carlin & Company of Brooklyn. This Romanesque gateway at Sands Street was completed later in the year to replace the former York Street entrance. Relocating the entrance was not universally embraced, and indeed was hotly opposed by businesses around York Street for the obvious reasons.

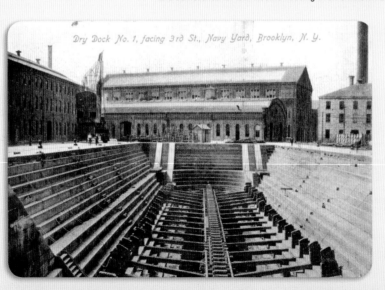

Dry Dock No. 1, facing 3rd St., Navy Yard, Brooklyn, N. Y.

◄ Famed warships built here included the battleship *Missouri*, on which the Japanese surrender was received at the conclusion of World War II, as well as her sister ship, the *Iowa*. Three post-war Forrestal class aircraft carriers were constructed here including the *Constellation*, launched in 1960, the largest of the Yard's production. The size of existing dry docks became a national concern in the late nineteenth century as modern vessels, notably battleships, became larger. No. 1 was a modest facility by the time of this c.1910 card, having been supplanted by larger examples. Following the closing of the Navy Yard in 1964, a variety of commercial/industrial tenants have located here and provided some revitalization, but the yard's post-navy incarnation awaits the opportunity to reach its full potential.

chapter five

Williamsburg & Greenpoint

The American Sugar Refining Company plant, which spanned four blocks of the Williamsburg waterfront from South 1st to South 5th Streets, was once the world's largest sugar refiner. It closed in 2003. The ten-story, 1884 main building, having lost the pictured pyramidal towers, is proposed to be preserved for adaptive use as residences and flanked with two forty-story residential towers. The building that stands to the right of this factory, erected after publication of this c.1905 card, is mounted with the familiar Domino Sugar sign, which has become a widely cherished, if not officially designated, landmark. This sugar giant was organized by Henry O. Havemeyer, less-known now as the sugar trust baron than for his magnificent art collection, much of which was given to the Metropolitan Museum of Art.

BROOKLYN EAGLE POST CARD, SERIES 17, NO. 101.
SUGAR REFINERIES ALONG BROOKLYN'S WATER FRONT.

◄ After Williamsburg and Greenpoint became late nineteenth century industrial centers, their populations soared with the opening of the bridge. While the many business buildings then along Kent Avenue reflected that commercial activity, they are gone a century later.

When the Williamsburg Bridge, the second East River crossing, engineered by ► Leffert L. Buck, which runs from Manhattan's Delancey Street to Washington Plaza, opened in 1903, it provided an exit path for Lower East Side residents, primarily Jews, who sought greener pastures, or at least a less-congested urban area, in Brooklyn. While the Williamsburg did not relieve Brooklyn Bridge traffic, the Manhattan Bridge, the third crossing, had already been in the planning stage before this bridge opened.

WILLIAMSBURG BRIDGE, N.Y. CITY

The Washington Plaza landscape on this c.1910 real photo card remains readily recognizable a century later — as every major structure is in place, including both of the domed bank buildings, the elevated railroad, and many surrounding, lesser-known structures. The ambiance, however, differs markedly as buses have replaced the trolleys while the plaza's northern section was chopped off by Jersey barriers that effectively make the Williamsburg Bridge approach a divided highway. At left, the former Renaissance Revival Williamsburgh Savings Bank, begun in the 1870s, reflects the 1906 George B. Post additions, including its massive dome with a faint resemblance to St. Peter's. The Plaza's namesake statue is actually mounted on the pedestal at the right, but is not visible due to a lack of contrast.

B 2484   NEW APPROACH TO WILLIAMSBURG BRIDGE, BROOKLYN, N.Y.

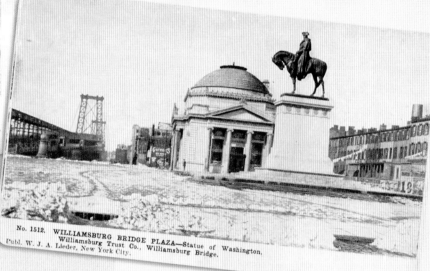

No. 1512. WILLIAMSBURG BRIDGE PLAZA—Statue of Washington.
Williamsburg Trust Co., Williamsburg Bridge.
Publ. W. J. A. Lieder, New York City.

Washington Monument, Brooklyn, N.Y.

The Classical Revival, inspired by the 1893 Columbian Exposition in Chicago, was utilized for artistic expression in bank design for at least a third into the twentieth century. Architects designed in the style to build substantial structures that conveyed solidity and financial security. Helme & Huberty designed this example for the Williamsburg Trust Company, completed in 1906 and pictured on a view looking west with South 5th and 4th Streets left and right of the bank respectively. The Washington statue setting, now a small park known as Continental Army Plaza, is separated from traffic by concrete balustrades.

Henry Merwin Shrady's equestrian statue, "Washington at Valley Forge," installed at the bridge plaza in 1906, is finely attuned to detail. His wrapped cloak and stern expression reflect the winter's cold. The tail between the horse's legs suggests wind while the legs are purposely made long in order to adjust the perspective while looking up. His lowered head helps the viewer see Washington. The First Presbyterian Church (Eastern District), organized in 1842, built the Greek Revival edifice in the background in 1848, which they sold to Trinity Methodist church in 1876. This building at 211 South 4th Street, at the northwest corner of Roebling Street, is now occupied, minus its portico, by El Puente, a community human rights institution that operates an academy for peace and justice.

▲ The Kosciuszko is one of New York's best known spans, although motorists stalled in traffic regard the bridge as more infamous than famed. Part of the Brooklyn-Queens Connecting Highway, which linked Meeker Avenue in Greenpoint with Woodside, the 6,025-foot Kosciuszkio Bridge with a 125-foot clearance over Newtown Creek is named for the Polish colonel military engineer who provided vital service during the Revolutionary War. Opened in 1939, the bridge is nearing the end of its useful life. A replacement was planned at publication. Bridges are a key subject in the oeuvre of Valeri Larko, whose specialty is the urban landscape, especially older and dismal parts, while at Newtown Creek, smelly can't hurt either. Her painting captures the view the motorist never sees — the perspective from the water.

▲ The digester tanks, or "eggs" in popular parlance, are the eye-catching structures of the Newtown Creek Wastewater Treatment Plant at 3239 Greenpoint Avenue between Provost and North Henry Streets. Designed by the Polshek Partnership, the first two of its ten 140-foot high and eighty-foot wide tanks began running in early May 2008. Artist Valeri Larko's specialty is her wide, deep, and varied output of industrial and urban scenes. While her eye is typically drawn to fading, decrepit subjects, the new tanks have a compelling character that draws one in. *Courtesy of Valeri Larko.*

◄ Elevated excitement and satisfaction swept through the crowd of several thousand when Mayor Seth Low laid the cornerstone of the Williamsburg Library on November 28, 1903. This branch represented the first of sixty that Andrew Carnegie promised the City of New York, of which twenty were to be located in Brooklyn. The Renaissance Revival design by Richard A. Walker, located at Division and Marcy Streets, is sited at angles to the street, perhaps to resemble an open book. The library, which opened in January 1905, remains in use today.

St. Anthony of Padua Roman Catholic Church, which was founded in 1856 and initially worshipped at a small building on India Street, erected this Gothic Revival edifice designed by Patrick C. Keely at 862 Manhattan Avenue, opposite Milton Street, 1873-5. Bishop John Loughlin laid the cornerstone on August 24, 1873, and returned June 13, 1875, for the dedication. Keely was one of the foremost proponents of Gothic architecture and utilized this as one of several basic designs in his enormous output: three doors on the façade with a center tower, usually finished with a steeple. A Second Empire rectory, which appears not infrequently with the Keely Gothic church of the period, stands adjacent on the south. The St. Anthony parish has been joined by St. Alphonsus Church. *Courtesy of Robert Pellegrini.*

▲ Holding for twelve years as unidentified, this real photo card made discovering its location during a field trip
▼ for this book quite satisfying. A walk along Norman Avenue while exploring Manhattan Avenue revealed a well-preserved early school there, one that instantly merited the taking of its image, which was later compared with the old card. The Renaissance Revival P.S. 34, now the Oliver H. Perry School, which fills the north side between Eckford Street and McGuiness Boulevard, was begun in 1867 and expanded in 1870 to designs by Samuel B. Leonard. James W. Naughton designed the wings, which were completed in 1888. Leonard and Naughton were each the principal architect of Brooklyn schools in their time. The 2010 photograph suggests little has changed on the façade. *Postcard courtesy of Joan Kay.*

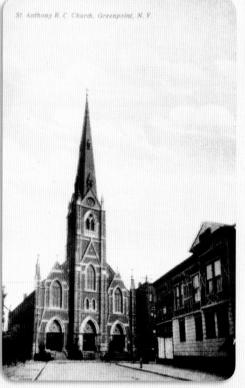

St. Anthony R. C. Church, Greenpoint, N. Y.

▲ The Brooklyn Diocese established national parishes in neighborhoods with significant ethnic populations and churches that drew worshippers from areas wider than traditional boundaries. In addition to St. Anthony, the significant Polish Catholic population of Greenpoint is represented by a second church, St. Stanislaus Kostka at 607 Humboldt Street on its southwest corner with Driggs Avenue. The massive, richly decorated Gothic church, several years in its construction, was dedicated by Bishop McDonnell on November 6, 1904.

Nassau Ave, bet. Humboldt & Russell St., Greenpoint.

▶ Built around 1869, the Greenpoint streetcar depot was located at 1119 Manhattan Avenue at Box Street. Surface lines often extended to city limits, which in pre-consolidation Greenpoint was Newtown Creek. A ferry from New York had been a long-time transportation alternative to reach Greenpoint. This route ended when it became the last East River ferry to terminate service on June 30, 1942. This building, and a number of adjoining structures, were destroyed by fire on June 30, 1952. *Courtesy of Joan Kay.*

The military function of the 47th ▶ Regiment Armory, built in 1883, is suggested by its resemblance to a fort, an impression reinforced by its crenellated towers. Constructed on the former Union Grounds athletic field, it stands on the block bounded by Marcy and Harrison Avenues and Heyward and Lynch Streets. The armory is now occupied by the 17th Corps Artillery. The c.1910 card was printed in England by Valentine and Sons.

▲ Postcards of infrequently illustrated neighborhood streets have an enhanced collector interest even when absent noteworthy subject matter. This c.1910 Nassau Avenue image, a street lined with simple frame buildings, is one such example. Most of these structures appear to have survived, but later cladding and remodeled storefronts obscure the present streetscape's past. *Courtesy of Joan Kay.*

◀ Hyde & Behman, which built the Folly Theatre in 1900 located at Broadway, Graham, and Flushing Avenues, operated it primarily as a vaudeville house. The intersection, now under the shadow of the elevated, remains a busy commercial-retail district 110 years later.

▲ Louis Bossert, born 1843 in Germany, began his career with a sash and blind manufacturer, joined his brothers in a similar venture, and took control of the firm after they retired. Their extensive plant, located at 8-30 Johnson Avenue, employed around three hundred and turned out a variety of interior woodwork. It was the largest of its type in the State of New York. The site is unrecognizable at publication, while Bossert, of course, is best-remembered for his namesake hotel pictured on page 23.

▲ The Wall Company used the back of this c.1910 card for advertising to make the claim that they were the largest stove and pipe repair house, and that they occupied this entire building, 60,000 square feet of a 100-foot square structure. Thus, one concludes their calculation included a basement. The Woodhull Medical Center, which uses an address of the nearby Broadway intersection, is on the site at publication.

The streets around the ▶ Brooklyn Griffin give vivid meaning to the term "gritty industrial area," but on a rooftop at the unlikely location of Waterbury at Scholes Street stands a nine-foot high, seven-foot wide robotic figure made from found objects by British artists who use the names Jimmy Bumble and Leonard White. This figure had its beginnings with salvaged parts from a similar piece that had an unhappy end following its uninvited mounting on what proved to be an inhospitable roof. While the Brooklyn Griffin, its informal name, may not have the durability of a museum bronze work, it is noted that beginning in 2010 there was exhibited an unlikely work in an unlikely Williamsburg setting.

◀ Ridgewood, a neighborhood bisected by the Brooklyn-Queens border, underwent intensive development in the two decades after the 1906 publication of this card. Its growth was aided by two streetcars and an elevated rail line. The latter reached the surface east of Wyckoff Avenue, the possible locale of this unidentified scene. *Courtesy of Joan Kay.*

Central Brooklyn

PROSPECT PARK

While Prospect Park is not a section or neighborhood, so-heading one of a small number of chapters that divide the borough for this book creates the opportunity to highlight the park and link places in proximity which enjoy the ability to walk there. Prospect Park, begun in 1866 in the midst of extensive farmland, became Brooklyn's crown jewel, an urban oasis in the center of brick and concrete, and, arguably the most satisfying accomplishment in the careers of designers Frederick Law Olmsted and Calvert Vaux. The park's topographical variety, its irregular polygonal shape and its diversity of spaces enhanced its endearment when regularly visited by the author.

The considerable foresight of the founders for setting aside 536 acres is recognized by the realization that urban parks at the time were more novelty than practice, but they anticipated the eventual growth of the city. The original layout included a section east of Flatbush Avenue, but a land exchange kept the entire park property west of that divide with the contemplation that this easterly section might be used for compatible cultural purposes. In time, that expectation was realized and provided homes for the Brooklyn Museum, the Brooklyn Botanic Gardens and the Brooklyn Public Library. The three organizations are critical part of Brooklyn's educational and cultural life. The Museum has outstanding collections that would be better known and even celebrated if located anywhere else but in the shadow of Manhattan counterparts. The Gardens has a strong education program. The Library is a center if culture, as well as the owner of a substantial Brooklyn collection of books, pictures and other material.

One early beneficial by-product of the park's establishment was the development of the Park Slope neighborhood, which, soon after it was begun, attained ranking as a competitive home site for Brooklyn's more affluent classes. While that area declined as a consequence of the urban ills that impacted many neighborhoods in the mid-twentieth century, Park Slope bounced back to regain its early and preeminent stature. The park itself has also recovered from periods of municipal fiscal neglect. Allowed to deteriorate during the financial crises of the 1970s, Prospect Park, aided by heightened local and municipal awareness, and assisted by support organizations, has become as well as ever fixed in public consciousness as Brooklyn's greatest open space asset. The park was entered on the National Register in 1980.

FLATBUSH

Flatbush is an Anglicization of a Dutch term with many variant spellings that means wooded plain. It is the center of Brooklyn, a large territory with shifting contemporary boundaries and several charming historic enclaves. The transformation of Flatbush from a farming community to a major residential and business section occurred just before and during the postcard era's golden age, so the process is well-represented in this graphic medium.

Flatbush is bisected by one of Brooklyn's longest thoroughfares, Flatbush Avenue, a street that was transformed from a narrow toll road to a major commercial stem. The area retains a major landmark denoting the section's former status as an independent municipality, the Flatbush Town Hall at 35 Snyder Avenue, located a block east of Flatbush. The avenue is also home of two of Brooklyn's greatest and tradition-bound institutions, one ecclesiastical, the other educational. The Dutch Reformed Church and Erasmus Hall are each described adjacent to their illustrations. The neighborhood, in its broad make-up, was also home to the Brooklyn Dodgers, long and popularly described as Flatbush based. Admittedly changing neighborhood lines deem their former stadium grounds as now in Crown Heights, while its proximity to Prospect Park resulted in the stadium being pictured in that chapter. In an era prior to city planning and local zoning, Flatbush was home to a number of real estate developments that became communities. They were organized by developers who wrote deed restrictions in order for them to retain their intended high-quality character. Today collectively known as Victorian Flatbush, a number are depicted in illustrations including Ditmas Park, Prospect Park South, and Fiske Terrace.

chapter six
Prospect Park

The oval Prospect Park Plaza, designed by Frederick Law Olmsted and Calvert Vaux and built in 1870, was intended to be both an entrance to that park and a connector of the major thoroughfares around it. Prospect Park West is in the foreground of this northeasterly view, in which Eastern Parkway recedes in the background and Flatbush Avenue between them is concealed in the trees. The library was planned for the southerly side of the Parkway corner while much of the thoroughfare was destined for the apartment houses that in time lined the street.

Brooklyn, N.Y. Defenders Arch Entrance to Prospect Park.

The quadriga is titled "The Triumphal Progress of Columbia" while The Army is subtitled "Genius of Patriotism Urging American Soldiers on the Victory." Its companion is "The Navy, American Sailors Boarding a Vessel at Sea Urged On by the Genius of Patriotism." Wayne Craven indicated the army piece resembled Rude's Le Depart on the Arc de Triomphe, which was not far from MacMonnies' Paris studio, while the less-chaotic naval piece is reminiscent of Franklin Simmon's relief to the Republic in Portland, Maine.

DEFENDERS' ARCH, PROSPECT PARK, BROOKLYN, N. Y.

▲ Two fine bas-relief equestrian sculptures reward the visitor who ventures inside the arch. Pictured is the Abraham Lincoln by famed painter Thomas Eakins, which rests opposite a Ulysses S. Grant by William O'Donovan; both were installed in 1895.

▲ The Soldiers and Sailors Memorial is a huge cube that measures eighty feet high and eighty feet wide and contains a fifty-foot high arch. It stands in the southerly end of the plaza. The c.1905 card depicts the original name of Defenders Arch. The circle was renamed Grand Army Plaza in 1926 in honor of the Union forces of the Civil War. Some of Frederick MacMonnies' finest public sculptures are mounted here, notably the huge quadriga (four horses abreast) on top, installed in 1898, and figures representing the army and navy on the sides.

◀ The 1932 Mary Louise Bailey Fountain in the northern section of the Grand Army Plaza oval is a collaboration of architect Egerton Swartout and sculptor Eugene Savage. The focal point is the pair of nude figures, a female representing Felicity and a male representing Wisdom, while Tritons and Neptune are placed around its base. The fountain, which was given to the city by Frank Bailey to honor his fountain-loving wife, underwent a costly restoration from 2002-6.

2105 – Water Tower and Entrance to Prospect Park, Brooklyn

◀ Four fifty-foot Doric columns, which were designed by Stanford White and completed in 1894, form an arc at the Plaza entrance to Prospect Park. They are surmounted by eagles by MacMonnies. White was also the architect for the two twelve-sided, temple-like gazebos.

Eastern Parkway and Water Tower Prospect Park, Brooklyn, NY

◀ King indicated that the Romanesque-style Mount Prospect water tower, which faced Underhill Avenue and was built of pink synthetic granite, received water from the Ridgewood Reservoir via a pumping station. The adjoining reservoir could store 1,000,000 gallons. This reservoir supplied the Prospect Park region as part of a major system that served the Ridgewood, New Lots, New Utrecht, and Gravesend sections. Construction was prompted by the agitation of locals dismayed by poor water pressure. The tower was designed by Thayer & Wallace, which worked in conjunction with chief water engineer Van Buren; construction was completed in 1894.

▲ Eastern Parkway, built from 1870-4 and the first of the three grand boulevards designed by Olmsted and Vaux, was little more than a stark landscape c.1900 at its western beginning. However, the viewer may imagine the row of apartments begun not long after publication of this c.1908 card and the later library in the foreground. The water tower, which dominated the landscape prior to its 1935 demolition, had an observation walk that afforded a view of the entire city. Mount Prospect Park, which opened on the site in 1937, separates the library and the Eastern Parkway entrance to the Brooklyn Botanic Gardens. Surrounding development and mature trees, however, have taken away the ancient vista.

▼ The plans for a central library on the southeast arc of the oval that were announced in 1914 would have resulted in a massive Classical Revival/Beaux-Arts structure, one that would have made a suitable accompaniment to the Brooklyn Museum. Its construction began and then lagged, but a wing on Flatbush Avenue was completed in 1919. The building project, which was revived in the 1930s, resulted in a new Art Moderne building designed by Alfred Morton Githens & Francis Keally that is positioned with Flatbush Avenue on the right and Eastern Parkway on the left. The early chrome card, c.1940s, specified that is was made with a Kodachrome image, makes one lament the loss of this all-time great color slide film, which Kodak stopped producing in 2009.

CENTRAL BUILDING, BROOKLYN PUBLIC LIBRARY

Kodachrome by Irene Strauss

Water Works. Brooklyn. N.Y. (57)
7-2-08 new york city

47784

▲ The *Times* prompted the reader on July 12, 1914: "No visitor to the Eastern Parkway district could fail to be impressed with its desirability as a home locality. Of high elevation, with splendid streets, open spaces and well-built homes, it presents all the charms of open-air living close to and easily accessible to the business centers of Brooklyn and Manhattan." The row of fine apartments on the north side, east of the Plaza, is pictured on a 1930s linen, albeit a dismal one that hardly merits similar praise.

People-watching is an active and well- ▶ known aspect of New York City apartment living. Architect Richard Meier's 2009 "On the Park," well, near the park, anyway, at the north side beginning of Eastern Parkway, creates vast new opportunities. The coverings on its glass walls, ranging from non-existent to full, would appear to be part of the appeal, one that gives new meaning to the adage "people who live in glass houses…" The library is in partial view at the right while the General Slocum monument, poorly-contrasted amidst the greenery, is on the left.

▲ The scale of the forty-foot high limestone pylons at the entrance, pictured in 2010, is suggested by the adjacent figures. They and the doors were well-described by Christopher Gray in his July 25, 2004 "Streetscapes" column: "…flanking 40-foot high limestone pylons covered with gilded relief carvings from the arts and sciences. The sculptor C. Paul Jennewein combined modern figures, including a miner and an electrician, with classical ones, among them Athena and Zeus. Centered within the pylons are huge bronze gates with gilt figures of literary subjects – including Tom Sawyer and Moby Dick – designed by Thomas Hudson Jones." The library was listed on the National Register of Historic Places in 2002.

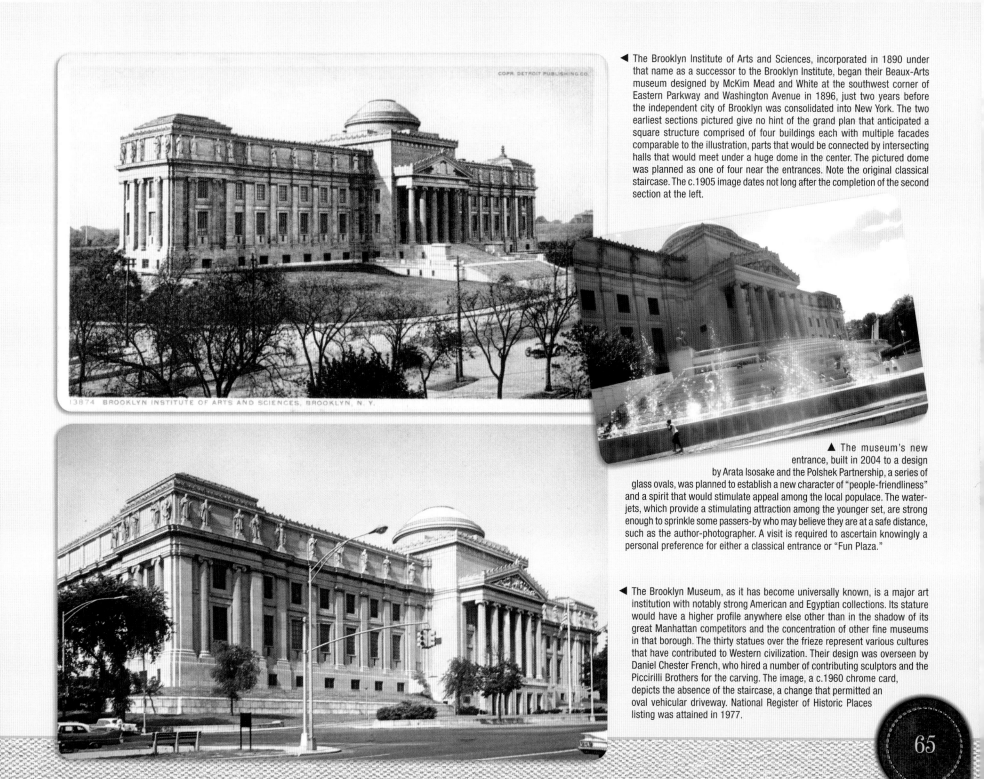

The Brooklyn Institute of Arts and Sciences, incorporated in 1890 under that name as a successor to the Brooklyn Institute, began their Beaux-Arts museum designed by McKim Mead and White at the southwest corner of Eastern Parkway and Washington Avenue in 1896, just two years before the independent city of Brooklyn was consolidated into New York. The two earliest sections pictured give no hint of the grand plan that anticipated a square structure comprised of four buildings each with multiple facades comparable to the illustration, parts that would be connected by intersecting halls that would meet under a huge dome in the center. The pictured dome was planned as one of four near the entrances. Note the original classical staircase. The c.1905 image dates not long after the completion of the second section at the left.

COPR. DETROIT PUBLISHING CO.

13874 BROOKLYN INSTITUTE OF ARTS AND SCIENCES, BROOKLYN, N. Y.

The museum's new entrance, built in 2004 to a design by Arata Isosake and the Polshek Partnership, a series of glass ovals, was planned to establish a new character of "people-friendliness" and a spirit that would stimulate appeal among the local populace. The water-jets, which provide a stimulating attraction among the younger set, are strong enough to sprinkle some passers-by who may believe they are at a safe distance, such as the author-photographer. A visit is required to ascertain knowingly a personal preference for either a classical entrance or "Fun Plaza."

The Brooklyn Museum, as it has become universally known, is a major art institution with notably strong American and Egyptian collections. Its stature would have a higher profile anywhere else other than in the shadow of its great Manhattan competitors and the concentration of other fine museums in that borough. The thirty statues over the frieze represent various cultures that have contributed to Western civilization. Their design was overseen by Daniel Chester French, who hired a number of contributing sculptors and the Piccirilli Brothers for the carving. The image, a c.1960 chrome card, depicts the absence of the staircase, a change that permitted an oval vehicular driveway. National Register of Historic Places listing was attained in 1977.

2. 21. 07.

Washington and Classon Ave. Flatbush, Brooklyn, N.Y. is hue leaves today
Dear Ella Letter receive to day Van fair is
for Washington will be table Sat night. He is having a good
time Sat Bye

▶ When collected and reclaimed architectural elements were placed at the south or parking lot entrance of the Brooklyn Museum beginning in the early 1960s, they were displayed in a manner not unlike a stone yard. These pieces were appealing, although they were little-studied, but over the decades appreciation for such discarded building elements grew and the grounds were given the design and care of a sculpture garden. The collection's most eye-catching item stands in the parking lot. It is a thirty-foot replica of the 151-foot Statue of Liberty, which was commissioned around 1900 by Russian-born auctioneer William H. Flattau. The galvanized sheet steel and zinc piece, which was affixed to an iron frame and fabricated in Akron, Ohio, stood for many years atop the eight-story Liberty Warehouse at 43 West 64th Street, New York. Concern was raised for the survival of this piece as the building's demolition neared because the replica had become a landmark in its own right.

▲ The c.1905 undeveloped state of the Washington (left) and Classon avenues intersection would be unimaginable a few decades later. The Brooklyn Museum was already erected, although off the left side of the image. The park that was built in the triangle was initially dedicated to Joseph A. Guider, born in 1870, who served as borough president 1925-6 and died in office September 22, 1926. His monument still stands, but a second was erected to rename the park for Dr. Ronald McNair, the first African American astronaut who was killed in the *Challenger* space shuttle disaster of January 1986.

▲ The Brooklyn Botanic Gardens, once part of the Brooklyn Institute of Arts and Sciences, dates from 1910 when begun on a former park system ash dump located next to the Brooklyn Museum. Its long-serving first director, C. Stuart Gager (1872-1943), established a grounding in plant education, which included a number of public programs, and was responsible for this Cranford Memorial Rose Garden, which opened in June 1927, and the two gardens that follow herein.

▲ The Japanese Garden, one of the most tranquil places in the Botanic Gardens, was designed by Takeo Shiota in 1915. Pictured in the spring of 1966, the hill and pond garden, which incorporates four styles, was maintained for many years by Japanese landscapers.

◀ The Botanic Garden's grove of cherry trees, one of the largest in the country, is a sea of pink each spring.

South Entrance, Prospect Park, Brooklyn, N. Y.

47791

▲ Prospect Park's south entrance is Park Circle, or the juncture of Prospect Park Southwest with Parkside and Coney Island Avenues. McKim Mead and White designed the pedestals (1897) on which are surmounted Frederick MacMonnies' "The Horse Tamers," a sculpture originally exhibited at the 1901 Pan-American Exposition in Buffalo. Wayne Craven wrote of this piece, "The nude athletes, who strain every muscle to control the mighty beasts they ride, represent the triumph of the mind over brute force, again an attempt to depict an abstract concept through a symbolic, but naturalistic, image."

▼ Calvert Vaux designed several rustic shelters that surrounded the lake. As they were built partially of logs, their durability may have provided challenges. One can presume that this boathouse was a predecessor of the adjacent pictured example.

▲ The Prospect Park Zoo, a later replacement of the 1890 menagerie, was built in 1935 with Works Progress Administration funds. Its well-designed six structures, by architect Aymar Embury II, are set in an oval. Their aesthetic appeal is enhanced with murals and reliefs that were executed by the program's artists. Buildings in a significant state of deterioration and concerns over constrained space for the animals led to the zoo's closing in June 1988. The zoo underwent total reconstruction and, as a consequence, rededication on October 5, 1993, as the Prospect Park Wildlife Conservation Center. The zoo has long-been a crowd pleaser, notably the seals that, even in the old enclosure pictured on a c.1940 linen, swam, sunbathed, and cavorted to the delight of all.

Prospect Park Lake, which ▶ enjoyed immediate popularity with boaters, is the site of this Renaissance Revival boathouse, designed by Helmle & Huberty and built in 1905-6. While this c.1909 Valentine & Sons card conveys an image of solidity and durability, a half-century later the structure was so deteriorated that it was threatened with demolition. Preservationists mounted a persistent campaign in the 1960s, maintaining their advocacy for its care even as the price tag rose. Their efforts convinced the city to finance a lengthy and costly restoration. Subsequently, the boathouse was rededicated in 1972 prior to its reopening in 1974.

New Boat House, Prospect Park, Brooklyn, N. Y.

Lake and Boathouse. Prospect Park, N. Y.

The Parade Grounds, located adjacent to the park on the south side of Parkside Avenue at Park Circle, became an effective annex when designated in 1868 as a place where Civil War veterans could hold military exercises. This exclusionary gesture was intended to keep marching, as well as noisy sports out of the park proper, as these activities were deemed of a lower and unfitting character for the attitudes of the day about park use. While this card designates the 1905 Georgian Revival design of Helmle, Huberty, and Hudswell as the Parade Ground House, the sports' building has been called other names, but by usage, it was the "athletic building." It was demolished in 1962 for replacement by a new police precinct and recreational center.

Scene in Prospect Park, Brooklyn, N. Y.

▲ Olmsted and Vaux designed five arches that served not merely as passageways, but as places of respite, rooms with seating where the walker could seek relief from the sun and his exertions. They include the pictured Nethermead Arch. Their architectural substance notwithstanding, they receive little respect, not from this c.1905 publisher who merely labeled this example "scene"; not from the public, notably the vandals that add their painted "artistry"; not from the city, which is challenged to maintain them; and not from collectors who disdain park cards. In his July 17, 1994 *Times* "Streetscapes" column, Christopher Gray said of the Nethermead: "The low triple span threads a bridle path, a stream and a pedestrian pathway underneath a set of catacomb-like brick and stone vaults. These evoke the sense of a Seine bridge or the gloomy romance of a Poe story."

▼ Over the years the Shelter House has alternately been called the Croquet Shelter, or the Grecian Shelter, as the Neo-Classical structure takes inspiration from a Greek temple. This 1906 project of McKim Mead and White employs twenty-eight Corinthian columns to surround a terra-cotta balustrade over a full entablature. Pictured on a real photographic card c.1915, the shelter, which faces Parkside Avenue, was restored in the latter 1960s and again in 1999-2000. It and the boathouse were entered on the National Register in 1972.

The Tennis Pavillion. Prospect Park. Brooklyn, N. Y.

SHELTER HOUSE PROSPECT PARK BKLYN   713

◄ Tennis courts, as many as three hundred at the peak, were built in Prospect Park to respond to the great late nineteenth century boom of the sport's popularity. Olmsted chose the location of the tennis house adjacent to the west side of the Long Meadow in 1894, well-prior to its construction. This Renaissance and Beaux-Arts influenced tennis house, designed by Helmle & Huberty, was finally completed in 1910.

The Vale of Cashmere was planted with a variety of flowers and became a center for bird-watching. Barely discernible, right of center, is the MacMonnies fountain of a boy who holds a duck that spouts water from its mouth.

The Shepherd and Herd in Prospect Park, Brooklyn, N.Y.

◄ What has become known as the Long Meadow was earlier called the Sheep Meadow, which in its day was actually a pasture for the woolly creatures. The herd, maintained by the park, became popular with children and artists alike. The Long Meadow, near the park's western edge, is an eighteen-acre, .75 of a mile open green belt, which is said to be the lengthiest open expanse of parkland in the country.

Henry Kirke Brown (1814-1886), a native of ▶ Chicopee, Massachusetts, opened a Brooklyn studio after studying sculpture in Italy for four years and became an American pioneer in the casting of bronze. An already existing War Fund Committee of Brooklyn, which had earlier resolved to honor the martyred president after the conclusion of Civil War hostilities, raised money through their "dollar subscription fund." This Brown Lincoln, which faces west at the formal Garden Terrace, is mounted on a Scotch granite base and points with his right hand to the *Emancipation Proclamation*. There are two eagles on the base: the one facing south holds a shield in the center in which a woman is holding an axe; the eagle on the north shows a broken shackle in his talons. The artist was present at a public ceremony on October 21, 1869, to unveil the statue. Brown has another major local public work — his equestrian statue of George Washington in New York's Union Square Park.

Lincoln Monument, Prospect Park, Brooklyn, N.Y.

Revolutionary Monument, Prospect Park, Brooklyn, N.Y.

63035

▲ This monument on Lookout Hill was erected in 1905 by the Maryland Society of the Sons of the American Revolution in honor of four hundred soldiers from that state and Delaware. While defending the rear of the colonial forces during the August 27, 1776, rout by the British during the Battle of Long Island, a debacle also known as the Battle of Brooklyn, the soldiers suffered great losses. Their valiant effort aided Washington's withdrawal, which helped preserve the battered and precarious American army.

MOUNT VERNON REPLICA, BROOKLYN – West Front

▲ The 1932 bicentennial of the birth of George Washington was a huge national celebration that marked the high point of the Colonial Revival, the cultural and artistic movement that celebrated our national origins and left an enduring manifestation on the landscape notably in the form of design motifs that expressed architectural interpretations of colonial-era buildings. Some entire period buildings were replicated for celebrations, including this 1932 Mount Vernon, which was designed by architect Charles K. Bryant and built by Sears Roebuck at the foot of Lookout Hill by the north end of the lake. Indeed, the Mount Vernon porch (on the façade not pictured here) is one of the most enduring architectural images of the Revival. Work began on February 26, two days before the ground-breaking event and was finished for a May 1st ceremony. The building, which some did not want to be placed in the park at all, became endeared to others who wished to see it preserved. However, it served one season only and did not open the next year; in time it was removed.

▲ Sculptors Augustus Lukeman and Daniel Chester French joined forces for the Prospect Park World War I Memorial, which is installed near the lake and off the concourse. The twelve-foot high granite ellipse, which measures thirty-five feet across, is mounted with panels that list the names of the Brooklyn war dead while, in front, the angel of death stands behind a doughboy. The memorial, a gift of William H. Todd of the shipbuilding firm, was dedicated June 27, 1921. It replaced a temporary wood memorial.

◄ Lawyer Edwin C. Litchfield, who made his fortune through owning railroads in the Midwest, purchased a square mile of vacant land in the 1850s that was developed into much of the future Park Slope. Alexander Jackson Davis designed for him this Italianate Villa house, built 1854-7 on the east side of Prospect Park West between 4th and 5th Streets. The Litchfield Villa, its best known name, has served as the Brooklyn headquarters of the New York City Department of Parks and Recreation for many years and was entered on the National Register of Historic Places in 1977.

259 The Montauck Club, Brooklyn, N. Y.

◀ Club life, which was important to the social structure of Brooklyn, had long-been centered in well-established Brooklyn Heights. However, the latter nineteenth century growth of affluence in Park Slope gave rise there to a new club whose founders demonstrated their stature by building an exuberant, richly-decorated clubhouse that has been aptly compared to a Venetian palazzo. The Montauk Club, named for Long Island's Native American tribe, hired Francis H. Kimball to design their Venetian Gothic headquarters, built 1889-1891, at 25 Eighth Avenue on its northeast corner with Linden Place. The first three floors were given over to dining and entertainment while the fourth and fifth floors contained members' residential rooms. The obligatory bowling alley was in the basement. While Brooklyn club life has evolved, the exterior of this brownstone, brick, terra-cotta, and verdigris copper remains unchanged, preserved and still-portraying the image on this c.1905 Rotograph card.

◀ Fitting the stadium designed by Clarence Randall Van Buskirk into this city block made for unusual outfield configurations. Center-field play was a challenge while the short right-field fence was a tempting target for left-handed hitters. The image's tint resembles a cyanotype of the early twentieth century, but this is actually a modern card with a picture of Game 1 of the 1949 World Series, which was published by the *New York Times* and distributed gratis to home-delivery customers.

◀ When Charles Ebbets broke ground for his new ballpark on March 4, 1912, he hoped to finish it in time to enable his team, then known as the Superbas, to relocate from Washington Park to play some late season games there. The 4.5-acre plot, bounded by Bedford Avenue (the destination of home runs that sailed over the short right-field fence), Sullivan Place, McKeever Place, and Montgomery Street, produced a small park, but one that was designed to be the most modern to date. However, construction delays resulted in postponement of its opening until April 1913. Brooklyn's strong identification with the Dodgers stemmed, in part, from the city's location in the shadow of Manhattan, for the intimacy of Ebbets' stands close to the playing field, and from the residence of many players in the community, especially during playing season. Thus, the collective community loss after they departed following the 1957 season was a massive, crushing blow; some have still not recovered. Ebbets Field was razed in 1960 to permit the construction of the Jackie Robinson houses now on the site. The white border card is c.1915.

Ebbet's Field, Brooklyn, N. Y.

ALTAR TO LIBERTY

▲ The William B. Cronyn House is two times a rarity; one, as a stand-alone residential survivor on a much-developed 9th Street, and second, as a private residence commission of Patrick C. Keely, the prolific ecclesiastical architect. The origins of the Second Empire house, a style Keely regularly employed for rectories, at number 271 suggests the 1870s, but the roof could be an addition to an Italianate house. The place, listed on the National Register of Historic Places in 1982, has interest for its post-residential incarnation when it was incorporated into the Charles M. Higgins Ink Factory plant, which, absent that occupant, remains in the rear of the lot. Higgins, an Irish immigrant, who made a fortune from an India drawing ink of his invention, was active in public and club life. He was an ardent supporter of the campaign to commemorate the Battle of Long Island, but his advocacy for a public park in its honor was unsuccessful. Higgins died in 1929 before the discovery of the remains of what became known as the Old Stone House. He did, however, pay for the statue of Minerva at Green-Wood Cemetery that honors the Maryland forces at that battle.

▲ Nicholas Vechte, who built what in time was known as the Old Stone House, sold to Jacques Cortelyou in 1790 the place that had been used as a headquarters by the American General Lord Stirling during the Battle of Long Island. In an era prior to the respect of historic monuments, the building was used as a clubhouse by the Brooklyn baseball team and in an era prior to the protection of landmarks, it was destroyed by vandals. Following the discovery of its ruins in the early 1930s, a replica was constructed by the city at the J. J. Byrne Playground in Washington Park and is open for exhibition purposes at 336 3rd Street.

◀ Charles M. Higgins expressed his commitment to commemorate the heroic Maryland forces that valiantly fought at the Battle of Long Island, with the most sincere expression of efficacy — money. He donated funds to erect this statue of the goddess Minerva, a nine-foot bronze figure by F. Wellington Ruckstull. It stands well-sited on Battle Hill with a direct line of sight to the Statue of Liberty, which she salutes as a "reciprocal monument." The battle is commemorated on its August 27th anniversary, also the anniversary of the 1920 dedication of this monument known as Altar to Liberty. The previously clear view, however, has been unfortunately marred by the recent erection of a building on Green-Wood's western edge.

▲ Richard M. Upjohn designed one of America's greatest entrance gates for one of its earliest and most artistic public cemeteries, Green-Wood, which spreads over 478 acres at one of Brooklyn's highest points. Opened in 1840, Green-Wood erected this Gothic Revival portal to its main entrance at Fifth Avenue, opposite 25th Street, in 1861-5. Green-Wood, a forerunner in the movement for the cemetery as a beautiful park, was regularly used for recreational and leisure activities in an era prior to the existence of public parks. Its monuments are particularly rich in their broad representation of Victorian era funerary practices while Green-Wood's interments reflect a "Who's Who" of that period and beyond.

◀ The Egyptian Revival, while a minor, curious architectural movement during the Victorian era, has been utilized for some of its finest artistic expressions in cemeteries, notably entrance gates. Christian images predominate at the entrance to the small, but striking pyramid with sphinx at the VanNess-Parsons mausoleum, where the entrance is flanked with St. Joseph and the Virgin Mary holding the infant Jesus.

▲ The Green-Wood Chapel, a rich Beaux-Arts design by Warren and Wetmore, was built around 1910 adjacent to a hill that is noteworthy for its built-in vaults. Located a short distance from the main entrance, the chapel is open for prayer and contemplation as well as services. Its moving interior is richly decorated with stained glass. Green-Wood was entered on the National Register in 1997.

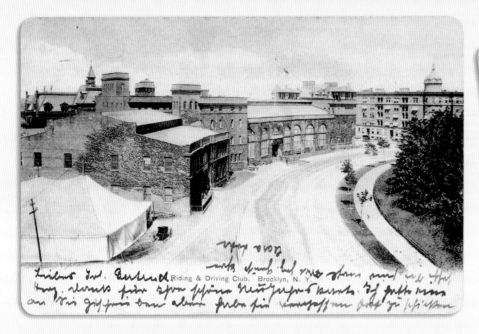

Riding & Driving Club, Brooklyn, N. Y.

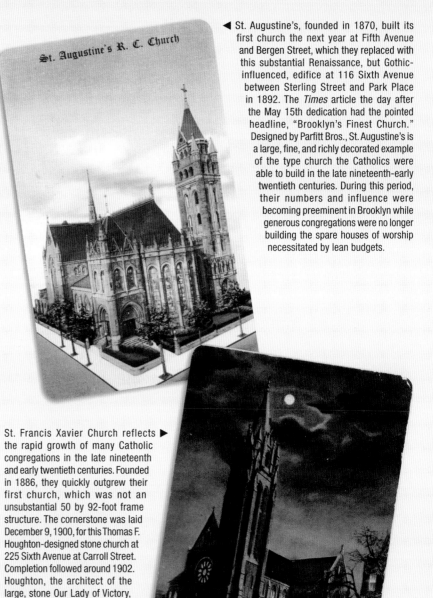

St. Augustine's R. C. Church

▶ St. Augustine's, founded in 1870, built its first church the next year at Fifth Avenue and Bergen Street, which they replaced with this substantial Renaissance, but Gothic-influenced, edifice at 116 Sixth Avenue between Sterling Street and Park Place in 1892. The *Times* article the day after the May 15th dedication had the pointed headline, "Brooklyn's Finest Church." Designed by Parfitt Bros., St. Augustine's is a large, fine, and richly decorated example of the type church the Catholics were able to build in the late nineteenth-early twentieth centuries. During this period, their numbers and influence were becoming preeminent in Brooklyn while generous congregations were no longer building the spare houses of worship necessitated by lean budgets.

▲ The Riding and Driving Club, organized in 1889 and often categorized as an athletic organization, was as much a social club that promoted riding and driving, which, of course, then meant horses and carriages. The *Eagle* of January 2, 1898, commented about their 95 by 190-foot headquarters at the Flatbush-Vanderbilt meeting with Park Circle, "While not particularly attractive on the outside, the club house is admirably suited to the needs of the club," such as being able to stable two hundred horses. Riding and Driving was a pioneer in women's rights, giving them equal privileges with the men and admitting them as active members if there was no male representative of the family in the club.

Organized in 1895, Troop C ▶ completed in 1904 this armory at 1579 Bedford Avenue between President and Union Streets following their occupancy of quarters at North Portland Avenue. Troop C, a crack cavalry outfit led by Major Charles I. Debevoise, was expanded to attain status as Squadron C by the armory's opening. The architects, Pilcher, Thomas & Tachau, designed a huge, arched roof structure that was not only a nod to the European Victorian era train sheds that are still numerous in many European cities, but also enabled the planning of what was claimed to have been the largest drilling floor in the country — an arena 818 feet long and 176 feet wide. The formal opening on April 11, 1907, was attended by Mayor George B. McClellan and a wide representation of local military. The place is now occupied by the 42nd Supply and Transport Battalion of the New York National Guard.

TROOP C ARMORY, BROOKLYN, N. Y.

St. Francis Xavier Church reflects ▶ the rapid growth of many Catholic congregations in the late nineteenth and early twentieth centuries. Founded in 1886, they quickly outgrew their first church, which was not an unsubstantial 50 by 92-foot frame structure. The cornerstone was laid December 9, 1900, for this Thomas F. Houghton-designed stone church at 225 Sixth Avenue at Carroll Street. Completion followed around 1902. Houghton, the architect of the large, stone Our Lady of Victory, which was widely acclaimed in 1895, became the predominant architect of Catholic churches in Brooklyn by at least 1890, attaining stature previously held by his father-in-law, Patrick C. Keely.

St Francis Xavier Church, 6th Ave & Carroll St, Brooklyn, N.Y.

John D'Emic's used car lot was staged for the photographer c.1950. They formed an orderly row of vehicles while a colorist tinted them with eye-catching hues. These practices were intended to draw in the prospective buyer, but they also unintentionally give this linen card enduring collector appeal. Courtesy of Joan Kay.

JOHN D'EMIC — USED CARS — 32nd Street & 4th Ave., BROOKLYN, N.Y.
SOuth 8-1282-1283

The Classical Revival Prospect Park Branch ▶ of the Brooklyn Public Library, a Carnegie donation, built in 1906 at 431 Sixth Avenue, was renamed Park Slope in 1979. The façade is unchanged, prior to the place's temporary closure for renovations in October 2009. The card is a c.1909 Valentine.

Public Library, Prospect Park Branch, Brooklyn, N.Y.

▲ Prospect Hall, founded in 1892, built this handsome Beaux-Arts entertainment mecca at 263 Prospect Avenue, designed by Ulrich J. Huberty. This real photo card has a 1909 inscription, "Biggest hall for dancing in South Brooklyn," but its ornate interior was also the venue for a wide variety of musical entertainment. After a spell in decline and following extensive renovation, the place was reborn as Grand Prospect Hall. It is an elegant catering facility that received the honor of entry on the National Register of Historic Places. The building remains readily recognizable, despite having lost its pediment, apparently for a remodeling that added a floor. In modern times, the hall has been the site of numerous motion picture interior scenes. *Courtesy of Joan Kay.*

THE PILGRIM LAUNDRY, INC. PROSPECT & 11th AVES., BROOKLYN, N.Y.

◀ Pilgrim Laundry utilized a variety of advertising postcards for promotional purposes. This c.1950 example highlighted their employment, 550, of which eighty percent owned company stock, its location five blocks south of Prospect Park Southwest, and its customer base of 20,000. Commercial laundries were a regular presence on the urban scene in the era prior to widespread ownership of home washing machines. This linen card was strictly made for the firm's use, as evidenced by the mailer's permit printed "Paid" indicium in the usual position for the stamp. The building came down at an unspecified time at a now substantially changed intersection. *Courtesy of Joan Kay.*

chapter seven

Flatbush

This c.1890 image foretells the profound changes in Flatbush Avenue at the turn-of-the-twentieth century. Old estates were then being developed into housing while the street was in transformation into a major commercial thoroughfare. The image predates both the c.1905 card and the construction of the trolley. It reflects the old country path toll road character of the emerging busy shopping street. The toll collector's booth was relocated to Prospect Park. Courtesy of Joan Kay.

The Old Flatbush "Toll Gate", Flatbush L. I.

F. A. Lippold, 1120 Flatbush Ave., Brooklyn, N. Y.

THE ZABRISKIE HOMESTEAD and THE HISTORICAL OLD LINDEN-TREE over 225 years old, which stood opp. D. R. Church, on Church Ave., Flatbush L. I.

F. A. Lippold, 1120 Flatbush Ave., Brooklyn. N. Y.

▲ The Zabriskie House, on Church Avenue facing the Flatbush Dutch Reformed Church, had likely seventeenth century origins. After its destruction in 1877, the place and family were memorialized by Peter L. Schenck's *Historical Sketches of the Zabriskie Homestead*. This sketch of a classic Dutch style house with characteristic sloping eaves, which appeared in the book, was dated 1839 by Schenck. This c.1905 issue is an early example of the postcard as a historical souvenir.

◄ The Benjamin F. Stephens House was pictured in Ditmas, but little is known about it other than its location: 1284 Flatbush Avenue at the corner of Foster Avenue. The place is typical of the substantial Greek Revival houses built by the prosperous in the second-third of the nineteenth century. Stephens, a hydraulic engineer who built the Flatbush Water Works, also invented a hand vise and a well-digging machine. After he died there in 1903, his widow was still in residence at the publication of the Ditmas work, but the house was removed for development at an unknown date.

LLOYD'S MILL, FLATBUSH, L. I.

The Vanderveer House, which stood on the southwest corner of Flatbush ▶ Avenue and Avenue C, remained in that old Brooklyn family through the nineteenth century when it was last occupied by Peter J. Vanderveer and his daughter Mrs. L. C. Titus, according to the *Brooklyn Eagle* of July 16, 1899. The massive chimney on the western ell suggests that it is the original section of the house. Dormers are nearly always later additions in early Dutch houses while the pointed-arch window in the attic surely is as well. The "For Sale" sign on this c.1907 card suggests that the property was, by then, giving way to the avenue's development onslaught.

Old Vanderveer House, Flatbush, Brooklyn, N. Y.

▲ Lloyds Mill, also known as Zabriskies Mill, built in 1820 near the northeast corner of Erasmus Street and Nostrand Avenue, was distinguished by the rotary motion of its fans. While it was in use until mid-century, after the mill's function was superseded by tide mills at New Lots and Flatlands it was taken down in 1868. The provenance of the image is the aforementioned Zabriskie book.

RESIDENCE ON FLATBUSH AVE. BROOKLYN, N.Y.

▲ The second entry in the *Brooklyn Eagle's* lengthy look back at historic Flatbush on July 23, 1899, told the history of Melrose Hall, built in 1749 by Colonel Axtel, "an English army officer, a stanch (sic) tory and social magnate." The core of the house was about fifty feet square, but that was later disguised by a number of additions, including two major wings. The house had been moved back about four hundred feet from its Bedford Avenue location between Robinson and Winthrop Streets by Dr. Homer L. Bartlett. The place was named by the husband of a 1830s owner, the famous actress Anna Cora Mowatt, for its numerous rose bushes. In 1899, the house, vacant since the 1895 death of Dr. T. S. Drowne, was poised for development. It was known as Melrose Park several years later when this card, which shows new construction at its edges, was published.

◄ The Judge Vanderbilt House at Flatbush Avenue and Lincoln Road was built in 1876, according to Gertrude Lefferts Vanderbilt, who later resided here. The step-gables, which are reminiscent of houses in Holland, suggest an early expression of revival style house design that would become prevalent in the last quarter of the nineteenth and first quarter of the twentieth centuries. It was taken down, perhaps c.1920, for the development of apartments and stores now in the area.

An Old Homestead, Flatbush-Brooklyn. N.Y.

OLD VANDERBILT HOMESTEAD

Unidentified on this c.1905 ► illustrated card, the "old homestead" appears, from evidence in the Brooklyn Public Library photograph collection, to have been owned by Judge Lefferts Birdsall. Of estimated c.1800 origin, his residence was located on the west side of Flatbush Avenue opposite either Fennimore or Midwood Street. A 1914 image of the house, which shows it in deteriorated condition, suggests that it succumbed to development not long after.

▲ When the old Vanderbilt homestead was pictured in the Ditmas book, the picket fence and newer shrubs behind the fence suggested that the old farmhouse was still a residence. The house was of likely eighteenth century origin and was built with steeply sloping eaves that is a prominent characteristic of the Dutch style, but the center gable was a later addition. The house on Flatbush Avenue was occupied by a store a few years later.

Two large Colonial Revival houses, designed ▶ by George Palliser and built in 1899, stand out on a busy Ocean Avenue stem of the Ditmas Park Historic District. The corner house at 1000, the northwest corner of Newkirk Avenue, was erected for builder Thomas H. Brush. The view from Ditmas obscures the neighboring 1010, built for George Van Ness, a stockbroker who was apparently Brush's son-in-law. Palliser is best remembered for his late Victorian era house-plan books published jointly with his brother.

▲ Lefferts is one of Brooklyn's oldest families with late seventeenth century roots in Flatbush. Their house, which dated from that period, was burned, along with their crops, by colonial forces in the Revolution in order to deny them to the British. Rebuilt by the war's end, family members continued to live here until 1918. By then Lefferts Manor had been undergoing development for two decades. The old family homestead was donated to the city and relocated to the southern end of Prospect Park, where it now stands bordering Flatbush Avenue. The image is dated 1990. Their old burial ground is on a wooded slope in Prospect Park.

▲ When the Story brothers sold the Martense homestead at the southeast corner of Flatbush Avenue and Linden Boulevard to the Flatbush Trust Company in 1902, it was the residence of Rachel Martense, then age 101, who lived there with her nephew Joseph Story. The c.1905 postcard indicates she endured there for another three years. The façade seems to be a Greek Revival addition to a large Colonial era house. *Courtesy of Joan Kay.*

◀ The Flatbush Trust Company erected their banking building on the site of the Story house around 1905, about the same time the Flatbush branch of the Brooklyn Public Library was built around the corner on Linden Place. The new bank was founded in 1899 to serve an emerging Flatbush business community, especially on this main thoroughfare, in a section that was transforming its farms into residential developments. Around 1912, the bank was merged with the Broadway Trust Company, which, in turn, was absorbed into the Irving Trust Company around 1920. The building disappeared at an unspecified date. Built in 1905, the Flatbush Library pictured on Linden Boulevard is the original building designed by Rudolph L. Daus. It remains at the core of a building remodeled and expanded a number of times.

Flatbush Trust and Library Buildings, Flatbush, N.Y.

MIDWOOD CLUB.

David Clarkson, a substantial cotton broker and prominent social host, built this costly Greek Revival mansion around 1834 at Ocean Avenue, opposite Linden Street. The sixty-foot-square house was situated on a tract that extended east to Flatbush Avenue. When formed in 1887, the Midwood Club met at the Flatbush Water Company offices. It acquired the Clarkson house when the tract was bought by the Flatbush Park Association for development in the 1890s. Kenmore Place was cut through the tract. The Midwood Club could boast a prestigious Flatbush membership in its early years, but disbanded at an unknown date. The clubhouse, which underwent a change of occupants, was extensively damaged by fire in January 1940. Note the "For Sale" sign and the surrounding new construction in this illustration from Ditmas.

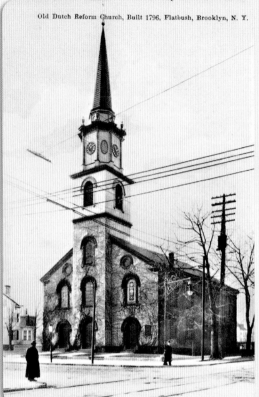

Old Dutch Reform Church, Built 1796, Flatbush, Brooklyn, N. Y.

The Flatbush Dutch Reformed Church at 890 Flatbush Avenue, its southwest corner with Church Avenue, was established in 1654 when it was the first of three mandated by Governor Peter Stuyvesant. A sparsely settled Flatbush at the time was served about monthly from visiting clergy from New York. The stone edifice of Manhattan schist, the third on the site, was designed by Thomas Fardon and built between 1793-8. It stands well-preserved, still reflects the character of this c.1910 card, and was entered on the National Register of Historic Places in 1983.

Flatbush and Church Avenues, which became one of Brooklyn's business shopping districts, is pictured looking north around 1930. Many of the buildings survive, but the change of signage and the commercial mix make the differences striking. The Zabriskie house would have stood off to the left.

Erasmus Hall, Brooklyn, N.Y.

The original Erasmus Hall, which is heralded as one of the oldest educational buildings in America, is a small, frame 1786 academy. Listed on the National Register of Historic Places in 1975, it is now located in the courtyard behind the 1903 Collegiate Gothic style Erasmus Hall High School. Designed by Charles B. J. Snyder, the latter building pictured on this c.1909 card stands on Flatbush Avenue at its southeast corner with Church Avenue. The older building now houses administrative functions and a museum. When the Academy's trustees anticipated the educational needs of a growing city, they donated the property to the City of Brooklyn in consideration of the establishment of a public high school. Snyder not only enjoyed a long career as architect to the New York City Board of Education, but he also advanced the science of school design. Many of his commissions are still in educational use.

303:—CHURCH AND FLATBUSH AVENUE, BROOKLYN, N. Y.

Flatbush Avenue, Flatbush, Brooklyn, N. Y.

▲ The northwest corner of Flatbush Avenue from Albemarle Road looking north, c.1909, shows an attached three-story row with bay windows on the upper floors, a type of structure extensively built in Brooklyn by the 1890s. The corner property survives, now accentuated by the dark green hue of its trim. Contemporary signage makes the rest of the row difficult to analyze, but some buildings of the same height appear to be replacements. Erasmus Hall High School on the east side is visible in the right background.

▼ This c.1905 Flatbush Avenue view north from Linden Boulevard remains recognizable from the retention of much of the built environment. Changes at grade, the cornice lines, and the disappearance of the four-story building in the left background, however, require a careful look.

4413   FLATBUSH AVE. LOOKING NORTH FLATBUSH, BROOKLYN, N. Y.

◀ The J. Harrison Furniture Company, written here with capital letters, his sign's Moderne style notwithstanding, looks appealing on a soft-colored linen c. 1940s that was probably stylized to remove residences above the store. His large Flatbush Avenue store south of Foster Avenue has since been broken into a number of smaller stores. *Courtesy of Joan Kay.*

◀ Flatbush Avenue is pictured looking south from Beverly Road around 1980. Photographer John Kowaluk made real photo postcards in the 1970s and 1980s in the manner of the c.1910 postcard era (although the camera was no longer likely to be aimed from the middle of the road). These cards were often overlooked when new, but many have acquired a vintage look as the cityscape evolves, but an unchanging corner sign makes this scene readily recognizable at publication.

◄ This Lincoln Road section on a c.1910 real photo card is probably the block east of Flatbush Avenue, which still retains a number of older frame houses. Note the gas lamp, which had to be lit manually. In the day, "lamplighter" was often a youth's first job. *Courtesy of Joan Kay.*

Cortelyou Club, Flatbush, Brooklyn, N. Y.

The firehouse at 1210 ► Cortelyou Road, which houses Engine Co. 281 and Hook and Ladder 147, was opened in March 1913, one of the first nine completed in a group of forty-six begun the prior year as part of a massive expansion of the City's fire-fighting capabilities. Much of the construction took place in areas developed as part of New York's post-consolidation growth. Design was intended to combine aesthetics with economy and suitability for the motorized apparatus that was then just emerging into regular use. The white border card is perhaps c.1915. *Courtesy of Joan Kay.*

FIRE HOUSE CORTELYOU ROAD, FLATBUSH, BROOKLYN N Y.

▲ The Cortelyou Club, organized in 1896, promptly built this Colonial Revival headquarters at 2581 Bedford Avenue, near Newkirk, which earned it the reputation as the pride of Vanderveer Park. Opened in 1893, Vanderveer Park was then a large neighborhood or development, but in the following decades it was absorbed by East Flatbush, Flatbush, and Midwood. The Club was formed by leading businessmen who had named it in honor of the old Brooklyn family that had earlier owned the tract on which their clubhouse stood. A c. 1910 postcard.

▼ Woodruff Avenue, which runs two blocks east from Parade Place to Flatbush Avenue, was lined with mature trees around 1910. Later apartment houses near the former have effaced any private residential character, but old private houses at St. Paul's Place are reminiscent of this real photo card. *Courtesy of Joan Kay.*

WOODRUFF AVE, LOOKING FROM FLATBUSH AVE, BROOKLYN

Knickerbocker Field Club, Flatbush, Brooklyn, N.Y.

▲ Founded in 1889, after the rapidly expanding Knickerbocker Club out-grew its modest clubhouse at East 17th Street and Albemarle Road, they built this Shingle Style-Colonial Revival headquarters adjacent to their tennis courts. The place was destroyed by arson in 1988, a time when the changing neighborhood was plagued with social and racial discord. The Club, once all-white but now integrated, built an open-air clubhouse that thrives once more. The Valentine & Sons card is c.1910.

▼ Many Ditmas Park streetscapes are little-changed a century after Ditmas' *Brooklyn's Picturesque Gardens*. However, Newkirk Avenue, a busy east-west street on its southern edge, underwent development. Thus, later construction has made many early street views there unrecognizable. The Ditmas Park Historic District was entered on the National Register of Historic Places in 1983.

Albemarle Road. Flatbush-Brooklyn, N.Y.

▲ Albemarle Road was planned as the main boulevard of Dean Alvord's approximate ten-block development of Prospect Park South. His marketing campaign, which began in 1899, sought "people of intelligence and good breeding." The street's main stem, east of Argyle Road, reflected Alvord's restrictions and was lined with numerous large houses that were primarily the Colonial Revival style and for the most part built in the first decade of the twentieth century. The appealing street, pictured looking east with 1519 Albemarle on the corner of Buckingham at the right, is divided by green islands said to have been inspired by Boston's Commonwealth Avenue. Albemarle remains a well-preserved exemplar of the Flatbush region. The Illustrated card is c.1905.

NEWKIRK AVENUE.

▲ Charles Ditmas identified the East 17th intersection, which made finding 1625 Ditmas Avenue a simple task. The house, which dates from around the turn-of-the-twentieth century, remains in fine, unchanged condition. Ditmas used the Albertype Company, a Brooklyn printer famed for "soft-color" postcards, for publication of his *Brooklyn's Gardens* book, which is comprised of hand-tipped prints produced in the manner of the firm's postcards.

Beverly Road, the northern boundary of Ditmas Park, runs east from Coney Island Avenue to Ocean Avenue and also forms the southern border of Prospect Park South. This c.1909 Valentine view, east from Albemarle Road, shows a well-preserved 1203 Beverly Road at the left.

RUGBY ROAD NEAR CHURCH AVENUE.

▲ The house with the step-gable is instantly recognizable as 94 Rugby Road. Its Spanish Mission Revival style was infrequently utilized in the east. Number 88 is behind it on a street developed c.1890s. The image is from Ditmas.

▼ Prospect Park South developer Dean Alvord intended that his Japanese-influenced house at 131 Buckingham Road be distinctive — and it has been since its 1903 completion. Designed by Petit & Green, the house, also reminiscent of the Stick Style from its exterior posts, received its first occupant in 1906: German radiologist Dr. Frederich Strange Kolle. The Japanese House, as the place is fondly known, remains instantly recognizable and still draws great interest for its unusual design.

▲ Buckingham Road was the alternate name of East 16th Street from Caton Avenue to Albemarle Road. The distinctive, little-changed Queen Anne style house is located at the latter street and is actually across the street from the Albemarle Road scene on the previous page. Automobiles, such as this one, were often added to card images by artificial devices around the 1915 period, but poor matching often makes their size seem grotesquely disproportionate.

The Japanese House, Flatbush, Brooklyn, N. Y.

BROOKLYN EAGLE POST CARD, SERIES 77, No. 457.
AVENUE G, LOOKING EAST FROM CONEY ISLAND AVENUE.

Westminster Road, Flatbush, Brooklyn, N. Y.

▲ Avenue G, now known as Glenwood Road, is the last in the sequence of the lettered avenues commonly known by a name with the exception of Quentin Road. The island remains, but commercial and apartment construction at the Coney Island Avenue corner overshadow the private residences.

Rugby Road, Fiske Terrace, Flatbush, Brooklyn, N. Y.

▲ Recognizable houses on both edges of this c.1909 Valentine & Sons card identify the Westminster Road scene as looking north from Beverly Road. It is the southern boundary of the Prospect Park South development begun by Dean Alvord in 1899, which included deed restrictions to ensure that large, quality houses were built in order to maintain its high design standards.

◄ The publisher of this c.1912 card not only added a crude depiction of an automobile, but labeled Rugby Road as Fiske Terrace. However, this street is a block west of T. B. Ackerman's c.1905 development that embraced the north-south streets of East 17th, 18th, and 19th. The *Times* claimed on March 19, 1905, when Ackerman made his purchase, that the tract was the highest elevation between Prospect Park and the ocean. This card, which depicts a solid row of Shingle Style and Colonial Revival houses, is a crudely printed American example of inferior graphic quality — the type that contributed to the decline of the era's postcard craze.

This Albertype view of a private residence at 494 East 18th Street, ▶ Ditmas Park, is an infrequent Brooklyn print example, as most such cards were the real photo variety. It was the home of Alexander C. Snyder, who enjoyed a long career as a banker and lumber dealer. Snyder died in 1923. His house, which combines elements of the Queen Anne and Shingle Styles, is unchanged and now is stained gray.

TENNIS COURT, FLATBUSH, BROOKLYN. N. Y.

▲ Richard Ficken developed c.1880s a high-class housing colony around its namesake street, Tennis Court, which runs the two blocks from Church Avenue and Albemarle Road. Ample lot sizes and a deed restriction that mandated costly houses were intended to maintain the development's high standards. The short street had a short life as the 1920s apartment house construction effaced any memory of Ficken's efforts. *Courtesy of Barbara Booz.*

▼ T. B. Ackerman's Fiske Terrace was named for the oil merchant George B. Fiske, who had sold him about thirty acres of his estate. Avenue H, the southern boundary of the small development, is on the bottom of this c.1910 northerly view. The house at left, 822 East 19th Street, remains readily recognizable, even after the enclosure of its porch, as are numbers 814, 810, and 804 above it. The quiet, well-preserved character of Fiske Terrace has resulted, in part, being designated a small historic district in conjunction with Midwood Park. *Courtesy of Barbara Booz.*

East 19th Street, Fiske Terrace, Flatbush, N. Y.

Ocean Ave, Flatbush-Brooklyn, N. Y.

▲ This Ocean Avenue view south from Church Avenue is a stem where its former private residential character was effaced by store and apartment construction, substantially in the 1920s. Illustrated Post Card Company, which published many series of numbered cards, later placed their numerals on the front. This is an earlier card with the numbers on the back. This example is No. 1 in their "155" Brooklyn series.

◄ Olmsted & Vaux designed Ocean Parkway, a six-mile boulevard that spans the edge of Prospect Park with Coney Island. The author's home for most of his Brooklyn residency, Ocean Parkway, is historically significant as America's first landscaped parkway that incorporates adjoining recreational space, its bridle, and bicycle paths on its east and west sides respectively. Service roads, as pictured in the lower right, separate local traffic from the main roadway. Construction began in 1874, with the Parkway opening two years later. One wonders how much change the writer of this card in 1906 had witnessed, but maybe "Edna" last drove there in the winter. The character of Ocean Parkway has evolved over the twentieth century to its present domination by apartment houses.

▼ The back of Collins' advertising card offered on his Caton Avenue strip, between East 3rd and 4th Streets, fireproof garages, seven rooms, bath with extra toilet, steam heat, parquet floors, and electric lights — all decorated to taste for $6,750. The row is little-changed at publication. The advertised private driveway runs the full block, on the north and behind the houses, and provides access to lower level garages. The card is c.1930. *Courtesy of Joan Kay.*

Caton Ave., Cor. Ocean Ave., Flatbush, Brooklyn, N. Y.

10039

MODERN ONE FAMILY HOMES

PETER J. COLLINS

▲ While most of the older side streets of northern Flatbush have retained their old private residential character, this fine Shingle Style house at a busy intersection reminds the viewer that even intensively developed Ocean Avenue once had a similar ambiance. Apartment houses now stand on all four corners. The white border card is c.1920.

B25:—BROOKLYN COLLEGE, BROOKLYN, N. Y.

48700

▲ Brooklyn College originated in downtown office buildings prior to building their campus at Bedford Avenue and Avenue H in the latter 1930s. The tract, earlier designated for a golf course, was offered to the city by architect Randolph Evans, who became the project's architect in association with Corbett, Harrison, and MacMurray after his ambitious proposal overcame hurdles through a lengthy approval process. The first buildings were organized in a U-plan: the library with a clock tower, LaGuardia Hall (for Mayor Fiorello), at the base and two academic buildings, Boylan Hall (for Dr. William A., first president) and Ingersoll Hall (for Ralph, borough president), on the sides. The linen card is a c.1940 view looking east, halcyon days when one could leave bicycles on Bedford Avenue.

ARTWIN MOTOR SALES, INC., 1249 CONEY ISLAND AVE., Corner Ave. I, Brooklyn, N.Y.

JOHN & ROSE—BEAUTY SALON—AIR CONDITIONED

1820 FLATBUSH AVE. NEAR K

MIDWOOD 8-5142

▲ Artwin Motor Sales' long Art Moderne building gives over half of this c.1940s linen to illustrate the Coney Island Avenue pavement. One wonders if they considered a split horizontal view image such as the automobile dealer example on page 51. At publication, a gas station is at this location on the east side of the avenue, a short distance south of the Long Island Railroad cut. *Courtesy of Joan Kay.*

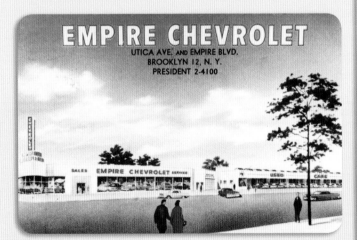

EMPIRE CHEVROLET
UTICA AVE., AND EMPIRE BLVD.
BROOKLYN 12, N. Y.
PRESIDENT 2-4100

SALES   EMPIRE CHEVROLET SERVICE   USED CARS

▲ The clean lines of the Art Moderne building and the apt use of color give the stylized drawing of this 1950s linen, a late example of the type, keen eye appeal. This card was posted by the dealer in 1965. The date of their departure is not known, but the building, actually closer to the intersection of Remsen and New York Avenues, is occupied as retail; a large drug store is at the corner. *Courtesy of Joan Kay.*

FLATBUSH OFFICE
GREEN POINT SAVINGS BANK
AT CHURCH AND UTICA AVENUES
BROOKLYN NEW YORK

⊗ GREEN POINT SAVINGS BANK ⊗

▲ Surely every postcard collector would like to confirm an appointment with a card like John & Rose's. The soft yellow and pale green coloration give it outstanding appeal and demonstrates why some linen cards are so popular. A fine Art Moderne interior was home to these "individual hair stylists" who were at the time "serving Flatbush patrons over 12 years," as was advertised on the back of this c.1940s linen. *Courtesy of the late Gary Dubnik.*

◀ While most of the commanding, eye-catching examples of Neo-Classical bank construction are high-design, even opulent structures, this Green Point Savings example demonstrates that the style could also be employed for a simple branch bank. When Green Point completed such a large bank at Church and East 51st Streets in 1937, the *Times* reported that it would replace an office across the street (or the pictured building). Note that Green Point, once one of the largest savings banks, originally split the neighborhood name into two words, which they, in time, changed. In 2007, they were merged into North Fork, which at publication is the occupant of the aforementioned larger bank. *Courtesy of Joan Kay.*

Business Section, Kings Highway, looking from E. 13th. St., to Brighton Beach Elevated

▼ The trolley line was replaced by an elevated subway line (no, that is not an oxymoron), which now runs along the former Gravesend Avenue. However, this scene at a Parkville western border with Borough Park is still recognizable, notably from the buildings in the center on the southwest corner of Eighteenth Avenue. Gravesend Avenue was renamed McDonald for John, a former Kings County clerk, while the aforementioned train is the Culver line, for Andrew, a former railroad and Coney Island developer. It is better known by its present incarnation as the F train. *Courtesy of Joan Kay.*

GRAVESEND AVE. & 18TH AVE., PARKVILLE, BROOKLYN, N. Y.

▲ While one can be tempted to perceive that the Kings Highway on this c.1907 easterly view was a quiet country scene, there is evidence of development that would turn it into one of Brooklyn's most vibrant shopping thoroughfares prior to the middle of the twentieth century. The street's changing character of recent decades leaves it with fewer of its former regional chains, but a greater number of ethnic stores.

The erstwhile Brighton line, which originated as the Brooklyn, Flatbush, ▶ and Coney Island Railway, has an open-air stem that gives it, in parts, the ambiance of a suburban railroad, especially the cut slightly under the surface. Since contemporary route designations often change, the line may still be remembered as its recent designation as the D train. At publication, it is the Q and B. Actually, old-timers may recall Brighton's first lettered designations, QB and QT; the former distinguishing the express train that traveled over the Manhattan Bridge while the local entered Brooklyn via an underground tunnel at lower Manhattan. The cut and the open-air Newkirk Avenue station were built during a 1904-8 project that elevated some sections as part of a plan to eliminate grade crossings. The underground sections were not completed until 1920, however. The station is undergoing reconstruction at publication, but is still recognizable, even after changes to the track crossing and its walkway. The station's best former feature was surely Ebinger's Bakery store, which was once on the northeast corner of its retail strip.

NEWKIRK AVE. STATION. BRIGHTON BEACH EL. 1907

Southern Brooklyn

BAY RIDGE

Bay Ridge in contemporary parlance embraces a wide area in southwest Brooklyn that may envelop adjacent Fort Hamilton and smaller surrounding neighborhoods. The region was largely rural until reached by the trolleys and notably by the Fourth Avenue subway. The name Bay Ridge comes from the area's geographical features, a hill adjacent to the bay, and replaced an earlier Yellow Hook, taken from the region's soil. The bay was once lined with estates and mansions along its shore road, the character so-well portrayed in the postcard era. A 1931 change in zoning led the way to its present streetscape lined with apartment houses. That fort is more than a footnote to contemporary neighborhood designation as it once mounted large guns and served to defend our coasts from naval attack. While that role was later surrendered to other forts before all such land fortifications were made obsolete by intercontinental ballistic missiles, an army base remains here.

In the late 1950s, Bay Ridge was threatened with a massive infrastructure project that had the potential to tear the neighborhood apart. The idea of the future Verrazano-Narrows Bridge was alien to the comfortable, well-established community, which viewed it and the resultant disruption as a need for the Staten Island side of the bay. Despite the destruction of many houses, the ripping up of numerous streets and the dismay of its then-residents, Bay Ridge survived and continued to be among the more appealing areas of the city. The local populace came to accept the bridge and, indeed, during an outward migration that began in the 1960s, many used the bridge as a springboard to residency in Staten Island and New Jersey.

CONEY ISLAND-GRAVESEND

Gravesend, as a chapter heading, stems from its historical significance rather than from having maintained its size, or familiarity, in current awareness. It was the only English town in greater Brooklyn and during English control that served as the county seat. It even lost that historic name on a major thoroughfare when Gravesend Avenue was changed to McDonald. Gravesend proper is even underrepresented pictorially herein. Gravesend did not particularly appeal to postcard publishers unlike the shorefront neighborhoods it spawned. Home to Lady Deborah Moody's 1643 settlement, Gravesend represented a safe haven when she and her followers were fleeing Puritan Massachusetts. They had great ambitions, although their achievements fell short of aspirations to make a major colony. Others also had great plans, such as those later in the nineteenth century who believed that there was potential for a seafaring port at Gravesend. However, the low water along the bay did not permit facilities for deep-draft vessels, but there was other waterfront opportunities in the area. When seaside entertainment and lodging were developed, a widespread following and even international fame came to the southern reach of the Gravesend area, the part known as the Coney Island section. This marsh was actually once an island, but later fill has made the territory a peninsula. While in popular parlance, Coney Island refers to the area's central amusement district. For practical and geographic purposes, the island extends from Sea Gate on the west to Manhattan Beach on the east.

Coney Island, a project long in the making, was hatched by John Q. McKane, a Sheepshead Bay carpenter who advanced through a number of local offices, in time attaining the power of political boss, authority that he wielded with abuse, in time becoming the region's despot, virtually a law unto himself. He met his comeuppance in the 1893 election in which his fraudulent activities were effectively prosecuted with a resultant jail term. His removal led to Gravesend joining Brooklyn in 1894. The Coney Island entertainment district was made by a number of pioneer amusement and hotel operators. The exploits and achievements of a number are outlined next to their illustrations, a space too brief to justify the impact Coney Island has had on New York's leisure life. At publication, success is threatening the traditional raffish make-up of the area as an emerging demand for better housing is pressing an economic squeeze on Coney's time-honored recreational occupancies.

chapter eight
Bay Ridge

Artist Thomas Chambers was born in London in 1808 and listed as a painter in New York City by 1834. He later spent ten years in Boston and about six in Albany, New York, before returning to the City. Chambers, who specialized in maritime subjects and marine landscapes, often painted from published prints. His *Staten Island and the Narrows* was based on an engraving published in 1840 in American Scenery. Brisk winds are suggested by the clouds and whitecaps in a view looking south through the mouth of New York Harbor. Chambers died in 1869. From the Collection of the Brooklyn Museum.

FORT LAFAYETTE DYNAMITE ISLAND OFF FORT HAMILTON, BROOKLYN, N.Y.

The construction of Fort Lafayette, earlier called Fort Diamond, two companion forts on the Staten Island side of the Narrows, and Fort Hamilton were prompted by the War of 1812, when the burning of Washington by the British revealed the vulnerability of our coastal cities to naval incursion. The substantial stone masonry fort, capable of mounting seventy-three guns, was made obsolete by increasingly powerful offensive weapons and later virtually useless after extensive fire damage. The former fort later served as a temporary prison. The "dynamite island" citation on the card may allude to two dynamite guns that were once mounted there. They were, as one might imagine, dangerous. The retired fort was later utilized for munitions storage, which was another controversial usage due its proximity to populated areas. The fort's shoal island, located on the site of the base of the Verrazano Narrows Bridge, was removed during the latter's construction. *Courtesy of Robert Pellegrini.*

While its cornerstone was laid in 1825 and the installation garrisoned in 1831, the fort, which was known from its early years as Hamilton, was not officially named for the former secretary of the treasury, Alexander Hamilton, until the twentieth century. Fort Hamilton played an important role in coastal defense during its early decades, but changes in both offensive and defensive weaponry later assigned New York harbor's principal defensive role to Fort Hancock at Sandy Hook, New Jersey. Famous officers who served here include Robert E. Lee and Thomas Jackson, the latter when a lieutenant long-before he became Stonewall during the Civil War.

WINT...

PARKWAY AND OFFICERS ROW, FORT HAMILTON, BROOKLYN, N.Y.

317:—GUN FROM FORT PITT AND WORLD WAR MONUMENT.

FORT HAMILTON PARK, BROOKLYN, N.Y.

The 51-foot obelisk at John Paul Jones Park, Fourth Avenue and 101st Street, is a memorial to the Dover Patrol and was erected as a tribute to the comradeship and service of the American naval forces in Europe during the World War. Unveiled on June 10, 1931, this monument, sponsored by public subscription in Great Britain, is identical to monuments that stand in Cap Blanc Nez, France, and Dover, England. The Rodman gun at the left had been the focal point of the park since the late 1890s.

Postcard publishers persisted in ascribing its origins to Fort Pitt, but its move from nearby Fort Hamilton was quite an undertaking itself. It is named for inventor Thomas Jackson Rodman, who developed a powerful, once state-of-the-art cannon, but its smooth bore barrel soon made it obsolete by new rifled guns that had greater accuracy and carried more destructive shells. The park is known on the street as "Cannonball Park."

▲ Some buildings of the fort have been adapted for use, but these houses were demolished and the street narrowed. A number of army units are based here, including the Atlantic Division of the U.S. Army Corps of Engineers. The army also maintains a harbor defense museum here. Fort Hamilton is a closed facility, which denies both the casual observer and historian the opportunity for personal inspection.

▼ Founded in 1834, St. John's Episcopal Church, at 9818 Fort Hamilton Parkway and 99th Street, built its first church in 1835, but now worships in this c.1910 edifice. In the shadow of Fort Hamilton, the numerous senior officers who have worshipped here have given rise to the popular nickname, The Church of the Generals. *Courtesy of Robert Pellegrini.*

▲ After decades of discussion, debate, and planning, the Verrazano Narrows Bridge opened in 1964 following five years of construction. Designed by the famed Othmar H. Amman, his eighth New York City bridge and one of his last works, the project was overseen by Leopold H. Just, who supervised over one hundred engineers and worked out details of its four main cables, each three feet in diameter, 3 million rivets, 1 million bolts, and 721,000 cubic yards of concrete. Calculations considered the curvature of the earth and the seasonal expansions and contractions of metal for a span that at 4,260 feet was the world's longest suspension bridge at the time. The view west looks at Staten Island, the borough that long-advocated for the bridge, which is pictured prior to completion. The continental-size card is deckle-edged, which to the author is an annoyance second only to writing on the picture.

Architect Raymond F. Almirall, impressed ▶ with the dome of Sacre Coeur when studying at the Ecole des Beaux-Arts, designed a fine copy on the tower of his St. Michael's Roman Catholic Church. Founded in 1875, the growing congregation built this Italianate edifice thirty years later at 4200 Fourth Avenue. This view of an unchanged church on a busier avenue is west from 42nd Street. *Courtesy of Joan Kay.*

◀ Founded in 1882, the Norwegian Lutheran Deaconess Home and Hospital, at 46th Street and Fourth Avenue, is pictured on a c.1910 real photo card. The street elevation suggests the west side of the avenue and the south side of the street. The deaconess movement, also practiced by the Methodists, included home health and social service care. A modern apartment fills that corner in 2010. *Courtesy of Joan Kay.*

BROOKLYN EAGLE POST CARD, SERIES 55, NO. 330.

BROOKLYN TERMINAL OF 39TH STREET FERRY.

▲ When the 39th Street Ferry opened, the *Brooklyn Eagle* waxed nostalgic on October 18, 1886, as they bemoaned that old South Brooklyn was gone for good. They lamented the loss of a number of landmarks, notably "Smedley's," which charmed the editors because this boat builder had managed to retain an old house and barn in the midst of his works. Real estate investors built the ferry because they expected property values to rise. They subsequently witnessed the local building boom with the area becoming more attractive as New York suddenly became much more accessible.

The Belt Parkway Showing Shore Road Drive, Brooklyn, N. Y.

▲ The Belt Parkway, earlier called the Circumferential Highway, was completed in segments during 1940-1. Both names imply its course around Brooklyn's western and southern edges. This late 1940s linen looks north towards the 69th Street Ferry to Staten Island, which closed within a week of the Verrazano Narrows Bridge's opening in 1964. Comparing this with an early twentieth century view of the area will show how part of the Parkway was built on filled-in land.

▼ The U.S. Army Supply Base was the largest of five planned in 1917 for the Atlantic seaboard for the storage and transport of supplies to France. The site, between 58th and 64th Streets from Second Avenue to the river, was chosen for its approximate one hundred-acre size, which was able to contain the largest of the facilities, and its availability for immediate development. Following the appropriation of funds in March 1918, work on the Cass Gilbert design began May 15, 1918, the date the contract was signed with Turner Construction Company. The project was completed in 1919, sometime later than it would have if the war had not ended the prior November. The floor area of all of the buildings is about 4,280,000 square feet, or ninety-eight acres, fifty-two of them in Warehouse B, which was said then to have the largest square footage in the world. If the measure was cubic capacity, it would be about equal to the Great Pyramid of Cheops. Entered on the National Register in 1983, the terminal is now occupied for various commercial and industrial uses. *Courtesy of Joan Kay.*

▼ Henry C. Murphy built Owls Head on his 125-acre estate overlooking the harbor. This house is a footnote to history because it was the site of a meeting on December 22, 1866, of Senator Murphy, William C. Kingsley, and Alexander McCue, in which an agreement to build the Brooklyn Bridge was reached. The image is from Stiles' "County."

20377 — The Tower, Bay Ridge, BROOKLYN, N. Y.

Shore Road from Crescent Club, Bay Ridge, Brooklyn, N.Y.

Shore Road from Crescent Hill, Bay Ridge, Brooklyn, N.Y.

SHORE ROAD, BROOKLYN, N. Y.

73rd Str. and Shore Road, Bay Ridge, N. Y.

Founded as a football club in 1884, the Crescent ▶ Athletic Club reorganized as an athletic club in 1886, incorporated in 1888, and soon took the character of a social organization for the elite. Their downtown clubhouse was located at Pierrepont and Clinton Streets and is partially seen on page 24. Sporting activities were centered at a country facility along Shore Road from 83rd to 85th Streets. The *Eagle* reported on January 2, 1898, that the Nereid Boat Club merged with the Crescent prior to the 1891 construction of that building, which cost $80,000. It was destroyed at an unspecified date. Fort Hamilton High School was opened on the site in 1941. This pictured boathouse stood opposite it.

◀ The construction of Shore Road was an enormous undertaking of the 1890s and required both legislation, notably for the city's acquisition of underwater lands, and a great outlay of money. J. S. T. Stranahan was an early advocate for such a road for the benefits that would accrue by opening up the region, but the timing was not right during his era a quarter-century earlier. The road's initial course was planned from 66th Street and First Avenue to run south to Fort Hamilton. Its varied elevation is suggested by the c.1909 Valentine card. At some points the road reaches a height of about seventy feet, but at other points it runs level with the water.

▲ The Owls Head property is more often associated with E. W. Bliss, a Brooklyn manufacturer who built this observatory tower that endured into the mid-twentieth century and outlasted the house. Though Bliss expanded his land holdings, after many years of discussion and planning, a smaller section was acquired by the city in the latter 1920s for Owls Head Park.

▲ This unidentified stem is one of the areas of Shore Road running along a higher elevation, pictured on a c.1910 card.

▲ This identified area of Shore Road, near 73rd Street, depicts a section close to the water. Compare it with the Belt Parkway image from the opposite page. A 1931 zoning change led to the construction of the apartment houses that later characterized and filled much of the road.

Shore Drive near Fort Hamilton, Brooklyn, N. Y.

▲ The Italian Renaissance Revival house at 9901 Shore Road, which was built around the first decade of the twentieth century by railroad investor Albert L. Johnson, is one of the few private residences of the era that still stands there. Its longevity can be attributed to its conversion to the Catholic girls' academic high school, Fontbonne Hall. The Sisters of St. Joseph, who bought the mansion in 1937, opened the facility that September. Fontbonne is the family name of Mother St. John Fontbonne, the founder of the order.

Shore Road at 92d St., Bay Ridge, Brooklyn, N. Y.

▲ The Spanish Mission Revival house at Shore Road and 92nd Street appears to date from the first decade of the twentieth century. The house's last incarnation was as the Shore Road Hospital, which was demolished in the late 1960s prior to the construction of senior citizen housing built there in the 1970s.

BROOKLYN EAGLE POST CARD, SERIES 79, NO. 474.

SHORE DRIVE LOOKING NORTH FROM NINETY-SECOND STREET.

▲ Bay Ridge is infrequently represented in the long *Brooklyn Eagle* series since the area was at the time less developed than the better represented northern parts of Brooklyn. Their card of Shore Road aids the viewer by identifying the street, enabling comparison at publication with high-rise apartment houses later built there.

▼ The designers of the Belt Parkway included recreation and rest areas on some shorefront sections. This late 1940s view is around streets in the 70s. It looks in a northeasterly direction and depicts the outline of lower Manhattan skyscrapers in the background.

Shore Road - Bay Ridge   Brooklyn, N. Y.

Photo - Rudy Larsen

This Sanctuary, a glory of colorful art and liturgical beauty witnesses the unending prayer of the Cloistered Sisters Adorers of the Precious Blood day and night.

◄ The two sides of the U-shaped structure, which faces the Parkway, are compatible but distinct, as comparison will demonstrate. This section adjacent to 54th Street is likely a later addition.

▲ The origins of the Monastery of the Precious Blood at 5300 Fort Hamilton Parkway stem from the 1889 arrival of the Sisters Adorers of the Most Precious Blood. This contemplative community, which is dedicated to prayer and penance, established a monastery on Sumpter Street the next year, outgrew both it and another downtown property before acquiring their present site in 1905, which spans the block from 53rd to 54th Streets. The new monastery was occupied December 3, 1910.

The back of this c.1930s card describes the bronze ▶ doors at the chapel entrance as a depiction of man's prayer and labor for spiritual and physical bread. At the left, the priestly spiritual father is sowing the seeds that bring souls to be fed at the Eucharist. At the right, the domestic father is sowing the seeds of labor to feed his family at home. The prayerful "May Jesus Mary Joseph be with us on our way" is printed on the back in the usual place for a stamp.

▲ Sandalphon, Masonic Lodge No. 836, built their hall around the turn-of-the-twentieth century at the northwest corner, which at publication is occupied by a business building of similar volume, one that challenges the eye to determine if it is an extensive remodeling or a replacement. *Courtesy of Joan Kay.*

97

▼ While Borough Park enjoyed rapid growth following its late 1890s development, other properties, still unbuilt c.1910, created anomalies where country scenes co-existed in the midst of new houses. Queen Anne was the style of choice then while deed restrictions banned flat roofs and two-family houses. The building at the right is apparently the school at 14th Avenue and 52nd Street. *Courtesy of Joan Kay.*

COUNTRY SCENE OF BOROUGH PARK AT NEW UTRECHT AVENUE.

FORTY-NINTH STREET RAIL-ROAD STATION, BOROUGH PARK, BROOKLYN, N.Y.

▲ When it was first developed, Borough Park was delineated as the tract lying between 40th and 64th Streets and New Utrecht Avenue and a line drawn two hundred feet east of 18th Avenue. The construction of 1,400 houses was anticipated on this tract of 5,400 city lots, which were sold with deed restrictions that required two lots for each residence, but five lots were mandated for 15th Avenue. The planners then designated 16th Avenue as the business street. *The Brooklyn Daily Eagle, June 4, 1899.*

▼ The character of 13th Avenue is so changed that this c.1910 scene is difficult to identify at publication. Now brick, multi-story buildings, many with commercial occupancies at grade, line the stem. The West End (B), elevated in the distance, suggests a location around 52nd Street, the view looking southwest. *Courtesy of Joan Kay.*

13th Avenue, Borough Park, Brooklyn, N.Y.

Our Lady of Perpetual ▶ Help, when founded by the Redemptorist Fathers in 1893, served a small section of Sunset Park. They bought the city block at 59th Street and Fifth Avenue, planned a larger edifice, and opened a lower or basement church in 1905, following a not uncommon practice of construction in stages to meet growing finances and following. Architect F. Joseph Untersee designed the Romanesque upper church (and signed the rendering), which was completed in 1928. The tall towers were never built. OLPH was inaugurated as a minor basilica on November 1, 1969.

CHURCH OF OUR LADY OF PERPETUAL HELP BROOKLYN

62nd St. Subway Station, Borough Park, Brooklyn, N. Y.

▲ A high concrete wall on 13th Avenue is an obstacle for the contemporary pedestrian who wishes to observe this c.1920s view. The Sea Beach cut, or N line in contemporary parlance, is pictured near the point where the elevated West End (B) crosses it at New Utrecht Avenue.

▼ The Bay Ridge Parkway is one of the early spacious Brooklyn thoroughfares. It formed the eastern boundary of Bay Ridge as it extended from Fort Hamilton Parkway to New York Bay, where it continues as Shore Road. At publication, the much-changed roadway is hard to identify as a consequence of the removal of its rural character by development.

BAY RIDGE PARKWAY, BROOKLYN, N. Y.

▼ The loss of character of some of the parkway roads in western Brooklyn has made identification of such scenes difficult. *Courtesy of Robert Pellegrini.*

View of Tunnel and Bridge, Bay Ridge, N. Y.

▲ This New York City Transit Museum card identifies the train as a BMT D-type Triplex and provides technical detail, but the old-time rider will remember them for their rattan seats and noisy operation. They ran until 1964 on the Sea Beach, Brighton, and West End lines, but the illustrated example was used for a nostalgia fan ride when it was pictured at Eighth Avenue on the Sea Beach (N) line.

Business Center—
5th Ave. and 69th St.

Bay Ridge Brooklyn
Photo—Rudy Larsen

▲ This 1948 view, north on Fifth Avenue from its northeast corner with Ovington Avenue, depicts a business block that has remained intact for over six decades. The Alpine Theatre still survives in 2010, as does the balustrade on the adjoining building on the corner of Bay Ridge Avenue. The Chinese restaurant is gone, although the nearby area now has a burgeoning Asian population. Its neighbor on the north became an Internet café, which may symbolize the meshing of modernity with stability.

▼ A round bas-relief of Abraham Lincoln, obscured by a shadow, identifies the former Lincoln Savings Bank on the northeast corner of Fifth Avenue at 75th Street, which is pictured looking north in 1948. The dates 1866-1934 is inscribed underneath Lincoln; the former likely marks the bank's founding as the German Savings Bank while the latter is presumably the date of the handsome Art Moderne building. The bank merged two years earlier with the Fort Hamilton Savings Bank, which had been located a block to the north. This active business street remains well-preserved over sixty years later, the contemporary scene changed only by evolving store fronts and signage. The trolley, of course, has long since been gone.

Bay Ridge Business Center
Brooklyn, N. Y.

Photo—Rudy Larsen

Public Library, 2nd Avenue and 73rd Street, Bay Ridge.
Brooklyn, N. Y.

▲ The Bay Ridge branch library was erected on Ridge Road's (the former Second Avenue) northeast corner with 73rd Street in the late 1890s, paid for by the local community. Thus, it preceded by a few years the neighborhood library construction boom funded by Andrew Carnegie. The building pictured c.1909 on a Valentine & Sons card was replaced by the present library built in 1959-60.

75th Street, looking East from Colonial Road, Bay Ridge, Brooklyn, N. Y.

◄ The transition of rural Bay Ridge to a suburb is symbolized by a c.1912 Valentine card view east. The large house in the center had been the seat of an extensive estate, but it was sub-divided around the turn-of-the-twentieth century. The Colonial Revival house at right, which was built around then, reflects Bay Ridge Park's prevailing standards of large lots, one hundred feet square on the corners, and were at times accompanied by deed restrictions requiring costlier houses. In time, smaller plots and multiple dwellings would dominate the area, as exemplified by the c.1920s six-story apartment buildings at 140 and 130 Bay Ridge Parkway that were built on the site of the larger house.

DUTCH REFORMED CHURCH, OVER 200 YEARS OLD,
18TH AVENUE AND 84TH STREET, BATH BEACH, L. I.

◀ The New Utrecht Reformed Church, which the A.I.A. describes as a Gothic granite ashlar church, is located on the south side of 18th Avenue between 83rd and 84th Streets and dates from 1828. Stone was recovered from the church of 1699 and utilized in the construction of this one. The church, which received National Register of Historic Places listing in 1980, has mounted a series of Liberty Poles dating from 1783, the year of the Treaty of Paris that brought peace to Revolutionary America.

▲ The suburban origins of this block of Bay Ridge Boulevard are evident on a c.1915 white border card. While many of the original private residences are preserved nearly a century later, a few masonry multiple dwellings were later built on this streetscape.

▼ The Marien Heim (home) for the Aged, pictured c.1905 at 18th Avenue between 64th and 65th Streets, was founded in 1895 by the German Ladies Association to provide a residence for their pensioners over age sixty. After they outgrew their initial quarters at Sixth Avenue and 46th Street, the Association bought the Lott Homestead and, according to the *Brooklyn Eagle* of October 22, 1901, were building at the time an addition at its rear. The image suggests that the original house is on the left while their addition is the larger three-story part on the right. The Marian Heim reported housing thirty-two inmates in 1902.

MARIEN HEIM,
EIGHTEENTH AVENUE, BROOKLYN.

▲ This unidentified house is the stylistic companion to the nearby Van Pelt house. One is not inclined to make a quick presumption of a family tie since its Dutch construction was widely built in any area with a concentration of Dutch settlers. The Washington tie is also obscure, if at all true. *Courtesy of Stan Lipson.*

101

The earliest Van Pelts in New ▶
York City date from the 1660s,
though the beginnings of the
family home that stood on 18th
Avenue at 81st Street may have
dated from later in that century.
Townsend C. Van Pelt was the last
family owner. The city acquired
the property after his death,
maintained it in the midst of a
playground for some years, and
then suddenly demolished it.

Van Pelt Old Homestead,
Built in the year 1664,
Bath Beach, N. Y.

▼ The 86th Street streetcar served Bay Ridge. While the open vehicle denotes the summer season,
note that the motorman is still bound in a three-piece suit and a high collar. Trolley accidents took
a significant toll in their early years. Thus, the safety poster cautioning one to wait for a stopped
car was good advice then and still, as stepping on or off moving trains presents a danger hazard
of which some travelers are still unaware. *Courtesy of Joan Kay.*

◀ Nostalgia envelops this Shore Road Fotoshop linen card. Many can remember when
one bought a camera at a shop from a dealer who instructed you on its use, a camera
that took film, perhaps in an era when a "Kodak" was a synonym for a camera. The
decorating style of the 1940s was to place as much of the store as possible in the
window. Even the graphics utilize a nostalgic typeface. Stores endure, although tenants
change. When the author last looked a decade ago, this was a cigar shop, but at
publication, a florist. *Courtesy of Joan Kay.*

8th St. Station, Bath Beach, Brooklyn, N. Y.

In the early years of the twentieth century, Bath Beach still retained the resort ambiance that for so long ▶
characterized much of outlying Brooklyn. However, that change was in the wind was suggested by a village
sprouting along the rails. The boundaries of Bath Beach in the nineteenth century were more extensive than
the present several blocks along Gravesend Bay. Before Bensonhurst was established, the last of the
farmer Bensons could declare, according to the *Eagle* of July 2, 1889, "Bath Beach shall come so
far and no further," as he expressed his intent to retain his land. However, after the sale of the
key Benson farm, development followed and Bensonhurst became densely settled.

L Station at Bath Ave., Bath Beach, N. Y.

It is believed that Bath's — its earliest references are without the Beach — date to the 1790s when a number of physicians who visited regional bathing places deemed this area on Gravesend Bay as possessing particularly healthful qualities for salt water bathing. The pictured train ran from Coney Island to Second Avenue and 38th Street.

The Avon Beach Hall has links to Bath Beach's earliest settlement, ▶ the time when several physicians built a boarding house in 1794 for the respite of their patients who were sent there for the supposed salubrious qualities of sea air. After that place was destroyed by fire, the property passed to Thomas Brown, whose hotel evolved into the Avon Beach. *Courtesy of Joan Kay.*

Kernan Avon Beach Hall, Bath Beach, New York.

Bath Ave. Bath Beach, N.Y.

◀ "The prime factor in the new growth of Brooklyn may be designated in one word — trolleys. The history of Brooklyn's latter-day development is the history of the Brooklyn trolley system," opined the *Eagle* on August 27, 1890. They added how the growth in Bay Ridge and surrounding environs had mushroomed in the four years since this trolley service was offered.

The Willomere. BATH BEACH, N.Y.

The early resort industry appealed to a wealthy clientele, but, by 1885, ▶ the *Brooklyn Eagle* of May 17th described the Bath Beach village as "a quiet, unfashionable resort...seldom if ever invaded by the class of people who visit that part of Coney Island which lies nearly opposite it." They appear to have been alluding to Sea Gate, which was developing along exclusive lines in that decade. Many Bath Beach hotels, such as the Willomere, hardly left a historical record. That remark also alludes to the link between travel access and the quality of the visitor. History demonstrates that ease of access and inexpensive transit lowered the social and aesthetic profile of early resorts.

chapter nine

Coney Island-Gravesend

PUB. BY   53
PHOTO. & ART P. C. CO. N. Y.

ENTRANCE TO DREAMLAND.
CONEY ISLAND.

Dreamland, built by politician William Reynolds in 1904, who also developed Borough Park, was the third of the three great early amusement parks to open; it was the best-designed and most beautiful, characterized by classical architecture and spacious grounds.

SHORE LINE, EAST FROM DREAMLAND CHUTES, CONEY ISLAND.

▲ The Leap-Frog Railway, pictured in the foreground, had two electric railroad cars speeding towards one another on a single track, although the name implies they avoided each other.

2060   THE TOWER BY NIGHT, DREAMLAND.
CONEY ISLAND, N. Y.

ILL POST CARD CO., N. Y.

◄ The 325-foot tower, which was modeled after one in Spain, was a bright beacon in the night sky. The proliferation of brightly-lighted amusement parks added both figurative and literal auras to Coney Island. The tower's publisher, Illustrated, issued night scene cards of Brooklyn landmarks that merely mar the image, but this one reflects the after-dark personality of Coney's great playground. Dreamland was destroyed in a spectacular blaze on May 26, 1911, which killed six babies in their display incubator.

THE CHUTES DREAMLAND   CONEY ISLAND

▲ The chutes at Dreamland may have been an early precursor to the virtually obligatory amusement park present practice of providing plentiful opportunities to get wet. It was arguably Dreamland's most popular ride.

◄ The 1955 New York Aquarium, at the Boardwalk and the northeast corner of West Eighth Street, was designed by Harrison and Abramovitz and built to replace the aquarium formerly at the Battery in lower Manhattan. It stands on the grounds of the former Dreamland and is pictured on a chrome card from 1964.

Bird's-eye View of Luna Park, Coney Island, N. Y.

▼ Luna Park boasted of stature as an "Electric Eden," a claim reinforced on the back of this c.1915 American Art card, which declared: "At night it is the most brilliant spot in Coney Island, being illuminated by thousands of electric lights." With what impression might the visitor leave? A friend's mother grumbled over wasted electricity and unused lights with the complaint, "Do you think this place is lit like Luna Park?"

▲ Frederick Thompson and Elmer Dundy's Luna Park, which opened in 1903 at Surf Avenue and West 10th Street, spread over enormous grounds and featured a variety of rides and entertainment. The place, according to Thompson's claim, employed upwards of 1,500 people and two hundred horses at its peak. Note the early version of an airplane ride at the right while the Scrambler at the left is a ride that seems to have a later, and still-surviving, incarnation as spinning cups. A glimpse of their water chute is in the background.

LUNA PARK AT NIGHT, CONEY ISLAND, N. Y.

AMUSEMENT BUILDINGS, LUNA PARK, CONEY ISLAND, N. Y.

◀ The exotic architectural design of Luna Park was intended to induce mirth, as exemplified by this row of amusement buildings that appear as if a line-up of wedding cake-like confections. Thompson loved minarets, spires, and towers, but avoided conventional forms and straight lines. Luna Park was substantially destroyed by fire on July 3, 1947, and closed permanently the next year.

▲ The Steeplechase, Tilyou's signature ride, mounted its passengers inside the pavilion on horses, originally made of wood, but later steel, and then took them outdoors on a rising and falling, curved course, prior to their return indoors. The proximity of a man and his sweetheart, with his gripping her on a shared horse, had a virtually erotic appeal in the dark ages where opportunities for physical proximity were scarce. Their personal delight would turn into public amusement as they left via a narrow corridor where bursts of compressed air would lift her skirt to the titillation of on-lookers.

▼ Steeplechase is pictured looking south from Surf Avenue towards the parachute jump along the Boardwalk, but their sizable swimming pool was left off the image at the right. This façade and the nearby entrance depict one of the amusement industry's most enduring, if not endearing, images, the Steeplechase Funny Face. Hardly charming, the author suspects most either love or hate it. Embarrassing the visitor was at the core of Steeplechase's fun ethos through the aforementioned air streams and other "tricks," which, while good-natured, might be no less humiliating, especially for the sensitive personality during a more genteel era.

▲ George C. Tilyou was not only the first to
▶ build his admittedly great Steeplechase Park, but he was also a master showman who produced the longest enduring of the three parks. Steeplechase also suffered extensive damage following a devastating fire in 1907, but was rebuilt. The divided back card pictures the new entrance. Note the signage, which includes a famed former Brooklyn beer and a photo studio, a shore resort staple. The photo of the family quintet in the prop automobile was made c.1910 in Wagner's Studios on the Bowery. They do not look happy, but a generation told to say "cheese" for the camera should be mindful this group was probably instructed to "freeze."

Charles Feltman, born 1841 in Germany, enjoyed immediate success at his 1874 stand for his ▶ "Frankfurt sausages." Burgeoning sales prompted him to open his huge Ocean Pavilion restaurant the next year. In time, it was transformed to his Deutschland Garden, which featured outdoor tables and singing waiters, a backyard ambiance that makes this 1930s linen of the once-familiar Surf Avenue façade prosaic by comparison.

FELTMANS   CONEY ISLAND

Wonder Wheel and Pony Track, Coney Island, N. Y.

◀ The Wonder Wheel at 3059 West 12th Street and the Boardwalk, invented by Charles Herman and installed around 1920, continues to be a wonder for having survived for nearly a century. Eight stationary cars circle the outer rim while sixteen cars pivot along the inner circle.

◀ Describing the old Coney Island subway terminal — where the West End, Sea Beach, Culver, and Brighton lines met — merely as "depressing" is relatively kind criticism. Welcome to the new station, which was completed in 2005 to a design by Kiss & Cathcart. Pictured looking north on Stillwell Avenue, the Surf Avenue façade with the old signage is both nostalgia and a prompt to old-timers that this is the same place they remember. One can almost become nostalgic recalling the old dim lighting, smells, dismal stores, and overall dinginess — an environment hard to imagine unless one was there.

◀ The Cyclone, which was invented by Harry C. Baker and engineered by Vernon Keenan, opened in 1927 at the southeast corner of Surf Avenue and West 10th Street. It survives, having attained stature as a cherished landmark and esteem as the quintessential Coney Island ride. The roller coaster boom of recent decades has reached new heights, literally, and marks for size, speed, distance, and action on the rail are measures that seem to be designed to test human endurance. However, the Cyclone endures because it is traditional and built of wood, the material of choice to coaster fanciers, stature that led to a National Register of Historic Places listing in 1991. Its setting is readily recognizable eighty-three years later and about fifty years after this c. 1960 chrome card, despite the disappearance of the entrance sign and some pictured surrounding features.

▲ The author acquired the Astroland cards at a time when the three-acre park was new, not having the slightest suspicion that it would endure to become the grand old dame of Coney Island. Most of the rides seemed tame while one might have expected its novelty space theme to wear thin. Yet it flourished and gained an enormous following. Some families claim three generations that visited as children. Attesting to its symbolic significance, when Astroland closed in 2009, some thought Coney Island had closed. Others merely felt as if a piece of their youth had disappeared. The view north from the Boardwalk shows Trump Village, named for developer Fred. Fred? He is the father of contemporary real estate mogul Donald and began developing Brooklyn real estate before his better-known son was born. Note the side view of the adjacent Cyclone.

▲ The roller coaster was invented by LaMarcus Thompson, who took inspiration from the Mauch Chunck, Pennsylvania, inclined-plane railroad and built his Coney Island structure in 1884. In the early years, they were often generically known as "scenic railroads." This unnamed ride appears to be an early version, as the circular type that returned riders to their starting point was an evolutionary improvement. Sterngass quotes *Frank Leslie's Illustrated Newspaper* of July 24, 1886: "The new Coney Island roller coaster is a contrivance designed to give passengers for the insignificant expenditure of five cents all the sensations of being carried away by a cyclone, without the attendant sacrifice of life and limb." Actually, safety was and is still an issue, especially since some riders revel in ignoring safety constraints.

◀ Astroland's 1962 opening had the good fortune to coincide with America's great early space-age accomplishment: *Project Mercury* Astronaut John Glenn's orbiting of the earth. The time was five years after the Soviets beat the United States into space with their *Sputnik* satellite, which shook our national confidence and heated up a space race that most Americans did not even know was taking place. The signature Astroland ride was its rocket, or Star Flyer, a 71-foot, 12,000-pound aluminum tube that took twenty-six earthlings on a three-minute simulated blast-off. The cable cars loosely resembled space capsules, at least somewhat more than did the typical ski slope versions. Atypical is the crane in the left foreground. After the end of the rocket's run as a ride, perhaps in the late 1970s, the spaceship was mounted on the roof of Gregory & Paul's restaurant as an advertisement.

▼ Prior to the 1922 season, the boardwalk was lengthened to two miles, widened to eighty feet at some points, and strengthened through reinforced supports — changes meant to enhance the appeal of the resort. Rock jetties were built to help prevent the washing away of sand. The Boardwalk, earlier administered by the Brooklyn borough president, was taken over in 1938 by the Parks Department, which was then headed by the powerful and influential Robert Moses. To improve a troublesome section, they relocated .75 of a mile of the boardwalk two hundred feet inland and added enormous quantities of sand to preclude tidal water from reaching the boardwalk. The rolling chair is so much associated with another eastern resort that many have forgotten that they also rolled along the Coney Island boardwalk.

The Tornado, originally called Bob's Tornado, is ranked among the three great Coney Island roller coasters along with the Cyclone and the Thunderbolt. It was designed by Prior and Church and built by the L. A. Thompson Company, a firm that survived by several years the 1919 death of the aforementioned inventor of the roller coaster, in 1927 near the Boardwalk east of Stillwell Avenue. It earned its claim of a "whirlwind ride" by virtue of configuration on a small, narrow lot that required numerous twists and turns in its track. The ride, actually cantilevered over Henderson's Walk, was also known for its one hundred-foot, well-lit tower. After the Tornado suffered a serious fire in December 1977, the remains were taken down the next year. The card is a 1940s linen.

This Surf Avenue night scene, c.1915, reminds that the Pabst organization, better known for Blue Ribbon beer, used to be a significant hotel operator. An amusement park staple in the old days was the entertainment versions of the "Wonders of the World," such as the Panama Canal and the replication of disasters, including floods and fires. The roadway was widened twenty feet in 1926-7.

The Reisenweber Casino, a branch of the famed nightclub on Columbus Circle in New York, stood on the corner of Ocean Parkway and Brighton Beach Avenue and included a restaurant. The New Brighton Theatre, designed by Dodge & Morrison (*Architects' and Builders' Magazine*, *Vol. XI*), was built around 1909 as a vaudeville house. It endured under other guises until demolished in 1955 to permit construction of an apartment house. The card is c.1910.

When Nathan Handwerker opened his stand in 1916, he observed that the traditional five-cent price of a hot dog had been raised to a dime, so he rolled it back to a nickel. Consequently, he built a business that not only dominated the Coney Island fast-food scene, long before that term entered our culinary lexicon, but, as the sign suggests, garnered an international following. Through franchising and supermarket sales there are, no doubt, Nathan hot dog fanciers who do not know the Brooklyn origins, let alone have seen an ocean. However, the special qualities of the corner of Surf and Stillwell made the experience at the place inimitable, including the noise, bedlam, and especially the smells. The image is a late 1950s chrome taken at a time when one could still spot a jacket and tie at Coney Island. Nathan's still feeds the masses, but now one can get frog legs and New England clam chowder here. Their coffee must truly be high-powered as the menu board listed it in the summer of 2010 as containing eight calories.

111

Scene on the Bowery, Coney Island, N. Y.

Commander James H. Strong invented a tower for use in training paratroopers, which he patented in 1936. However, its fame was garnered by amusement installations, first with a smaller one at a Chicago park and then this 250-foot high, twelve-chute example built for the 1939-40 New York World's Fair. After the Tilyous purchased it, the 170-ton tower was disassembled and re-erected at Steeplechase Park. There it thrilled and terrified the adventuresome for a quarter of a century, but after the park closed, the parachute jump became idle. There has not been an effective plan for its re-use, so now the parachute jump, entered on the National Register of Historic Places in 1980, has been unused for most of its time at Coney Island.

450 :- PARACHUTE JUMP AT STEEPLECHASE PARK, CONEY ISLAND, N.Y.

48220

Rumford Press, Concord, N. H.   OCEAN PIER AND WRECK OF "SARANAC."
Tilyou's Steeplechase, Coney Island, N. Y.   We are just going in bathing. Pier. M. C. J.

▲ The Bowery is a short side street that runs parallel and close to Surf Avenue from about West 12th Street to West 16th Street. While an absence of dignity is hardly reflected in this c.1910 view, the Bowery was often home to the unusual, the bizarre, and the freakish. A tight, narrow space accentuated the Bowery's noisy, raucous, and rough-edged character. When a "Waterboard Thrill Ride" opened on West 12th Street in 2008, one could wonder if turning torture into fun was a new low in poor taste or just Coney being Coney.

▲ While Brooklyn rail lines and street cars long brought most of its revelers, the introduction of regular steamboat service, aided by the construction of a substantial dock in 1879, expanded travel possibilities for those not already within reach of Brooklyn's (rail) cars. One can presume the *Saranac* was a minor vessel since it appears to have not been recorded on lists of wrecks or in the news.

112

Municipal Baths and Beach, Coney Island, N. Y.

Entrance to Sea Gate, N. Y.

▲ The municipal baths at Coney Island were, according to this c.1913 American Art Publishing Company card, "the largest and most sanitary bathing facility in the world." Two key qualities distinguished it from the other city public baths: it was not near a working class population center of regular users and it was not free. Located opposite West 5th Street, the baths, which opened August 1911, published rather exacting accommodation numbers of 5,533 men and 1,294 women. They charged a dime for a locker. Their fee dismayed advocates for the free usage that prevailed at other city baths.

▲ Nortons Point needed a major makeover to shed its reputation as a hotbed of vice and the home of gambling dens and bordellos operated by Tammany Hall politician Michael Norton. He thrived in the post-Civil War era as he drew a New York City clientele via steamships that docked at his namesake landing on the Lower New York Bay at the western edge of Coney Island. Developers renamed the area Sea Gate and literally installed an elaborate, Shingle Style gate house that gave New York City its first and still only gated community. After the pictured example was destroyed by fire, perhaps in the 1930s, it was replaced by a simpler utilitarian structure.

George B. Post & Sons designed the Spanish Colonial Revival Half Moon Hotel, ▶ built in 1927 at the Boardwalk and West 29th Street. The three hundred-room light brick structure had a roof garden and a plan that had the wings of its U-shape face the ocean, which maximized the number of water views. With the demolition of the hotel in 1997, a once-famed incident in New York crime annals may fade from memory. Here in 1941, Abe (Kid Twist) Reles, a protected prosecution witness in a case against Louis (Lepke) Buchalter, was being guarded by five New York policemen — yet still managed to fall or be pushed to his death from a sixth-floor window. The Half Moon's incarnations included a United States Navy convalescence center, which opened in 1942 and lasted through the war, and a Metropolitan Jewish Geriatric Center nursing home from 1954 to about 1990. The c.1930s card is a Lumitone, a publisher with an enormous output of New York hotel cards.

THE HALF MOON HOTEL, CONEY ISLAND, NEW YORK

The appealing Shingle Style Estes Lodge, which appears to date from the ▶ 1880s, gives the appearance of a small hotel or a large boarding house. The appeal of this real photo post card image notwithstanding, the place's history could not be found. However, it is a fine reminder of Sea Gate as a resort community. *Courtesy of Joan Kay.*

ESTES LODGE.
Sea Gate,
New York Harbor.

The Atlantic Yacht Club, located at the foot of 55th Street, built this Colonial ▶ Revival clubhouse in the 1890s, probably as a replacement of an earlier home. In its day, the organization was known for a prestigious membership; this place was destroyed by fire November 23, 1933.

Atlantic Yacht Club, Sea Gate, N. Y.

Boardwalk and Cottages, Brighton Beach, N. Y.

◄ Manhattan Beach reflected a Coney Island construction truism that, as one moved east, the quality and pricing of an area became elevated. Indeed, not long after its 1877 founding by Austin Corbin, this elegant seashore resort ranked with the finest in the east. His second success was the 1880 Oriental Hotel, which was demolished in 1915.

Brighton Beach Hotel, Brighton Beach, N. Y.

◄ Andrew Culver earned great profits from his Prospect and Coney Island Railroad. He desired to retain some of his passengers overnight, so he invested in the construction of the Brighton Beach Hotel, built around 1880. He claimed that it was the largest on the beach, an assertion supported by its huge 460 by 200-feet dimensions. After an eroding shore threatened to swamp the place, he moved the hotel back five hundred feet, a complicated project that utilized one hundred specially built railroad cars.

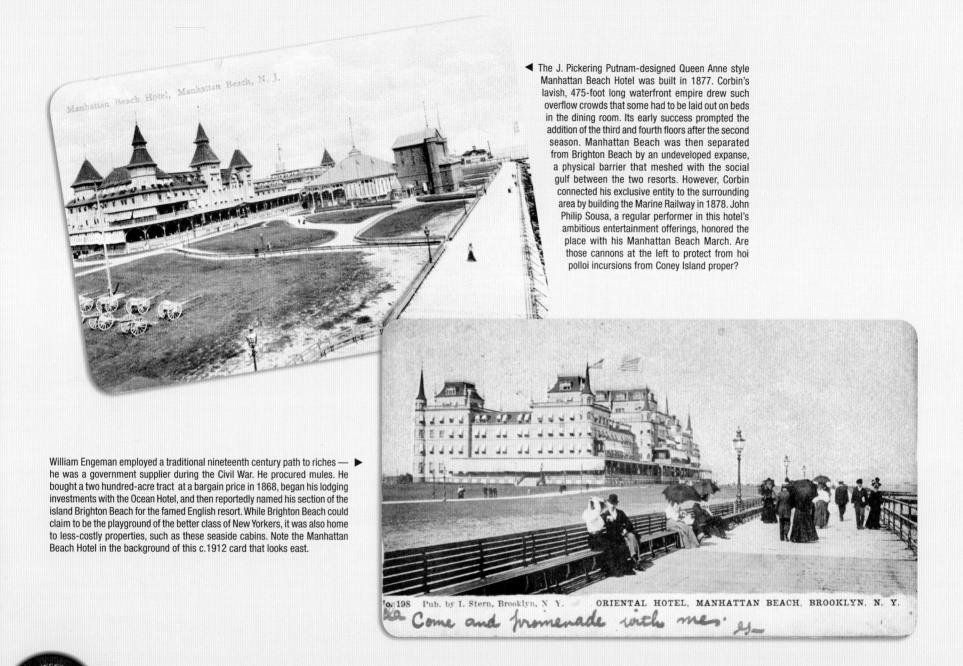

Manhattan Beach Hotel, Manhattan Beach, N. J.

◀ The J. Pickering Putnam-designed Queen Anne style Manhattan Beach Hotel was built in 1877. Corbin's lavish, 475-foot long waterfront empire drew such overflow crowds that some had to be laid out on beds in the dining room. Its early success prompted the addition of the third and fourth floors after the second season. Manhattan Beach was then separated from Brighton Beach by an undeveloped expanse, a physical barrier that meshed with the social gulf between the two resorts. However, Corbin connected his exclusive entity to the surrounding area by building the Marine Railway in 1878. John Philip Sousa, a regular performer in this hotel's ambitious entertainment offerings, honored the place with his Manhattan Beach March. Are those cannons at the left to protect from hoi polloi incursions from Coney Island proper?

William Engeman employed a traditional nineteenth century path to riches — ▶ he was a government supplier during the Civil War. He procured mules. He bought a two hundred-acre tract at a bargain price in 1868, began his lodging investments with the Ocean Hotel, and then reportedly named his section of the island Brighton Beach for the famed English resort. While Brighton Beach could claim to be the playground of the better class of New Yorkers, it was also home to less-costly properties, such as these seaside cabins. Note the Manhattan Beach Hotel in the background of this c.1912 card that looks east.

No. 198   Pub. by I. Stern, Brooklyn, N. Y.   ORIENTAL HOTEL, MANHATTAN BEACH, BROOKLYN, N. Y.

Come and promenade with me.

Brooklyn was the late nineteenth century regional center of horse-racing, a role shared with Jerome Park in the Bronx. Three tracks that operated in the southern portion of the city apportioned the season amongst themselves, including the Coney Island Jockey Club at Sheepshead Bay, the Brooklyn Jockey Club at Gravesend, and the Brighton Beach Racing Association in Coney Island. The L. Mauer painting *The First Futurity, Coney Island Jockey Club*, September 3, 1888, which shows Proctor Knott winning, as Salvator and Galen took place and show, is in the collection at the National Museum of Racing in Saratoga Springs, New York. ▶

◀ The Sheepshead Bay Race Track, part of a 430-acre tract at Ocean Avenue, south of Gravesend Neck Road, opened in 1880 and was esteemed as the best of the three. After anti-gambling forces ended racing in the early twentieth century, auto racing tried to take hold on the track in the years 1915-9. Following its failure, the park was razed around 1920. The large tract, which was held by real estate investors, was developed for housing after its 1923 sale by the Henry Sharkness estate. The Suburban's stature merited a card by a major publisher as it was arguably the nation's most popular race in its day. This still-run handicap race once had an enormous following that is comparable to the Kentucky Derby's in modern times.

SUBURBAN DAY AT SHEEPSHEAD BAY, BROOKLYN, N. Y.

▼ The Brighton line (Q), elevated at this point, is a visual reminder in a profoundly changed c.1910 Avenue U streetscape. Now the south side at the right is filled by three- and four-story apartments and stores. The taller building at the left had been a police precinct prior to the station's c.1980s relocation to Coney Island Avenue; the structure was later replaced by one-story stores. *Courtesy of Joan Kay.*

▲ Sheepshead Bay, a southern neighborhood that spread north from its namesake inlet, was both remote and sparsely settled until it was made accessible by latter nineteenth century rail lines and roads. It was a rural and maritime community until the city sponsored a 1930s upgrading of the area, which became home to a recreational fishing fleet pictured on this 1950s chrome. Post-World War II apartment construction so transformed the area that just the dock and their piers are left as the primary, if not only, reminder of the section's maritime roots.

AVE. U, EAST FROM E. 14TH ST., HOMECREST, BROOKLYN, N. Y.

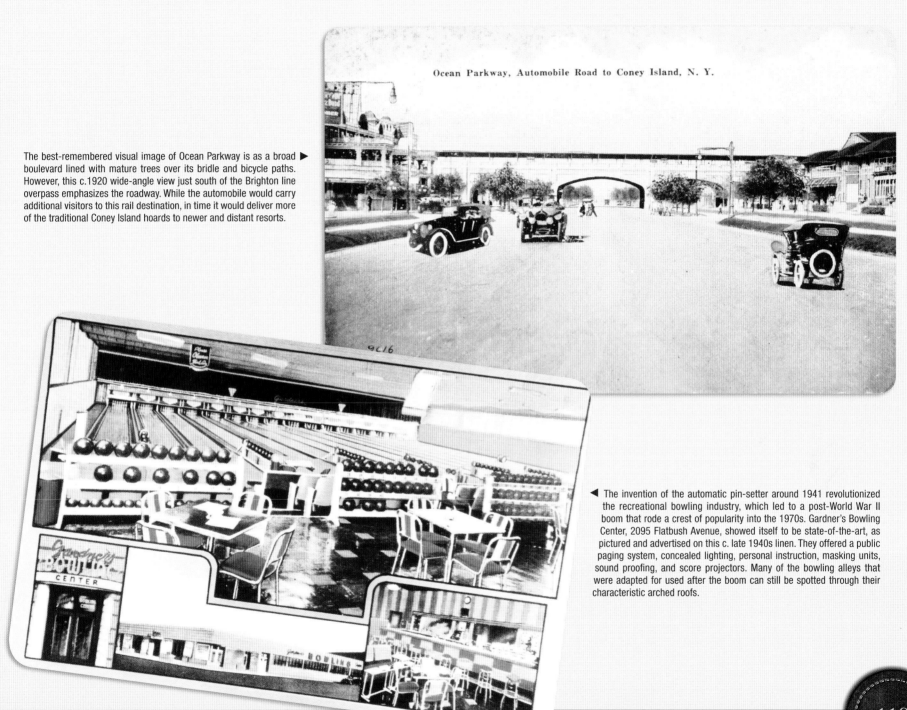

Ocean Parkway, Automobile Road to Coney Island, N. Y.

The best-remembered visual image of Ocean Parkway is as a broad ▶ boulevard lined with mature trees over its bridle and bicycle paths. However, this c.1920 wide-angle view just south of the Brighton line overpass emphasizes the roadway. While the automobile would carry additional visitors to this rail destination, in time it would deliver more of the traditional Coney Island hoards to newer and distant resorts.

◀ The invention of the automatic pin-setter around 1941 revolutionized the recreational bowling industry, which led to a post-World War II boom that rode a crest of popularity into the 1970s. Gardner's Bowling Center, 2095 Flatbush Avenue, showed itself to be state-of-the-art, as pictured and advertised on this c. late 1940s linen. They offered a public paging system, concealed lighting, personal instruction, masking units, sound proofing, and score projectors. Many of the bowling alleys that were adapted for used after the boom can still be spotted through their characteristic arched roofs.

Gravesend was founded in 1643 by Lady Deborah Moody, who ▶
led English Anabaptists fleeing religious persecution in Puritan
Massachusetts. They planned a four-square town center now
crossed by the present McDonald Avenue (nee Gravesend Avenue)
and Gravesend Neck Road. The early town plan can still be traced on
the contemporary streetscape through the modern street layout and
old burial grounds. However, there are few reminders of this ancient
settlement from the built environment and one is located at 38 Village
Road North: the Ryder-Van Cleef House. Note the characteristic flared
Dutch eaves in a house that was built in sections with the southern
part believed to date mid-eighteenth century.

◀ Crescent Street today is a long north-south
thoroughfare that runs from Cypress Hills·
Cemetery to a short stem of Flatlands
Avenue, but it had a creek outlet to the
bay before the marshes were filled-in. The
modest frame structures appear to reflect
typical waterfront life of the time. The
card is a divided back, but the message
border in the front suggest a pre-1907
image. *Courtesy of Joan Kay.*

The Marine Parkway-Gil Hodges Memorial Bridge had to overcome varied local opposition before construction was begun in June 1936. It is a four-lane vertical lifespan crossing of the Rockaway Inlet that connects Flatbush Avenue with the Rockaway Peninsula, designed by David Steinman and opened on July 3, 1937. The bridge proved an instant success that propelled the development of the peninsula and led to the construction of the Jacob Riis Park. Renamed in 1978 to honor Gil Hodges, the stellar Dodger first baseman, its 2,000-ton center lift span of 540 feet, which had a 150-foot clearance when raised, was the longest in the world at its completion. The charming color of this c.1940s linen mitigates its lack of sharpness.

362

MARINE PARKWAY BRIDGE, BROOKLYN, N. Y.

▲ Carman, an oyster fisherman who operated out of the Carnasie Bay section of Jamaica Bay and a location at East 92nd Street and Stillwells Lane, was apparently very successful. He was active at least since the 1890s. In 1914, when a proposed banning of oyster harvesting became a public issue, Carman claimed to make $50,000 annually. Additional information about the real photo image postmarked in 1908 is not known. *Courtesy of Joan Kay.*

140

FLOYD BENNETT FIELD, BROOKLYN, N. Y.

PHOTO BY RUDY ARNOLD

7A-H1758

◄ Floyd Bennett Field, which was New York's first municipal airport, opened in 1930 following construction on six hundred acres of reclaimed Jamaica Bay marshes. Bennett was celebrated at the time as Admiral Richard E. Byrd's polar pilot. Notable departures from this once-prominent airfield include the 1933 solo flight around the world by Wiley Post, Howard Hughes' record-breaking global circumnavigation in 1938 and, also in that year, Douglas Corrigan's flight to Ireland, which, after he announced his "intended" destination of California, earned him fame and the nickname "Wrong Way." Floyd Bennett Field was turned into the New York Naval Air Station in 1942, but its incarnation since 1972 has been as a unit of Gateway National Recreation Area and a National Register Historic District since 1980.

◄ At publication, Coney Island is threatened with the loss of its traditional character through gentrification.

Vaults in a hillside ► are an effective use of the topography at Green-Wood.

◄ The dome and classical entrance of the Dime Savings Bank building are among the best known images of commercial Brooklyn.

▲ A major commercial district arose around the ancient small houses on Duffield Street and the 1872 St. Boniface Church designed by Patrick C. Keely.

Roland at the library is ► requesting a copy of Dogs of Brooklyn.

We say goodbye to our Greetings with five contemporary images

Bibliography

This short list is representative of noteworthy in-print works in the author's library, which he consulted for this book.

Craven, Wayne. Sculpture in America from the Colonial Period to the Present. New York, New York: Thomas Y. Crowell, 1968.

Coulton, Thomas Evans. *A City College in Action – Struggles and Achievement at Brooklyn College, 1930- 1955.* New York, New York: Harper & Bros., 1955

Ditmas, Charles Andrew. *Brooklyn's Garden – Views of Picturesque Flatbush, Brooklyn.* Brooklyn, New York: Charles Andrew Ditmas, 1908.

Dutton, Richard L. Brooklyn – *The Brooklyn Daily Eagle Postcards* 1905-7. Charleston, South Carolina: Arcadia Publishing, 2004.

Fisher, Edmund D. *Flatbush: Past and Present.* Brooklyn, New York: Flatbush Trust Company, 1901.

Gabrielan, Randall. *Brooklyn, New York in Vintage Post Cards.* Charleston, South Carolina: Arcadia Publishers, 1999.

Glueck, Grace and Paul Gardner. *Brooklyn – People and Places, Past and Present.* New York, New York: Harry N. Abrams, Inc., 1991.

Jackson, Kenneth T., general editor. *The Neighborhoods of Brooklyn.* New Haven, Connecticut: Yale University Press, 1998.

Kelly, Wilhelmena Rhodes. *Bedford-Stuyvesant, Images of America.* Portsmouth, New Hampshire: Arcadia Publishers, 2007.

King, Moses. *King's Views of Brooklyn.* Boston, Massachusetts: no publisher, 1905; Reprint, Arno Press, 1977.

Lancaster, Clay. *Old Brooklyn Heights – New York's First Suburb.* New York, New York: C. E. Tuttle, 1961.

McCullough, Edo. *Good Old Coney Island.* New York, New York: Charles Scribner's Sons, 1957.

Morrone, Francis. *An Architectural Guidebook to Brooklyn.* Salt Lake City, Utah: Gibbs Smith, Publisher, 2001.

Snyder-Grenier, Ellen M. *Brooklyn – An Illustrated History.* Philadelphia, Pennsylvania: Temple University Press, 1996.

Sterngass, Jon. *Four First Resorts – Pursuing Pleasure at Saratoga Springs, Newport, and Coney Island.* Baltimore, Maryland: The Johns Hopkins University Press, 2001.

Stiles, Henry R., Ed. *History of the City of Brooklyn.* Brooklyn, New York: published by subscription, 1867-70.
> *The Civil, Political, Professional and Ecclesiastical History and Commercial and Industrial Record of the County of Kings and the City of Brooklyn, New York from 1683-1884.* New York, New York: W. Munsell, 1884.

Vanderbilt, Gertrude Lefferts. *The Social History of Flatbush.* Brooklyn, New York: Frederick Loeser and Co., 1909.

White, Norval and Elliot Willensky. *AIA Guide to New York City, 5th Edition.* New York, New York: Oxford University Press, 2010 (and prior editions).

Younger, William Lee. Old Brooklyn in Early Photographs 1865-1929. New York, New York: Dover Publications, Inc., 1978.

OTHER SOURCES

The Brooklyn Daily Eagle

The New York Times, notably the Sunday Christopher Gray "Streetscapes" column.

BROOKLYN EAGLE POST CARD, SERIES 34, No. 204.
MECHANICS BANK BUILDING, COURT AND MONTAGUE STS.

SHORE LINE, EAST FROM DREAMLAND CHUTES, CONEY ISLAND.

Ridge Boulevard East from 82nd St., Bay Ridge, Brooklyn, N. Y.

ARCH ON MONTAGUE St, BROOKLYN, N. Y.

29.99   10/11/12.